TEXTS ESTABLISHED BY THE LUXEMBOURG CONFERENCE ON THE COMMUNITY PATENT 1985

Council of the European Communities

This publication is also available in:

DA ISBN 92-824-0309-2
DE ISBN 92-824-0310-6
GR ISBN 92-824-0311-4
ES ISBN 92-824-0313-0
FR ISBN 92-824-0308-4
IT ISBN 92-824-0314-9
NL ISBN 92-824-0315-7
PT ISBN 92-824-0316-5

Cataloguing data can be found at the end of this publication

Luxembourg: Office for Official Publications of the European Communities, 1986

ISBN 92-824-0312-2

Catalogue number: BX-45-86-814-EN-C

© ECSC — EEC — EAEC — Brussels · Luxembourg, 1986

Reproduction is authorized, except for commercial purposes, provided the source is acknowledged.

Printed in Belgium

INTRODUCTION

On 7 October 1985 the Council meeting on the Internal Market invited the Presidency to call a Conference on the Community patent with the following triple objectives:

- the rapid implementation of the 1975 Luxembourg Community Patent Convention,

- the finalization of a Protocol setting up the judicial machinery for the settlement of litigation of Community patents, and

- the definition of the conditions governing participation in the system by countries which had acceded to the Community after 1975.

This Conference, comprising the delegations of the ten Member States of the European Communities, the two acceding States and the Commission, was held in Luxembourg from 4 to 18 December 1985.

As regards the rapid entry into force of the Convention, the Conference was unable to fulfil its terms of reference. It devoted its entire first part to innumerable attempts to overcome the difficulties presented by this problem. These difficulties were, however, eminently political and the Council meeting on the Internal Market on 12 December discussed the question at great length on the basis of an interim report on the Conference proceedings before concluding that the problem must be left on the table.

The Conference however succeeded in finalizing the Protocol on the Settlement of Litigation concerning the Infringement and Validity of Community Patents which provides a solution to the problem resulting from the separation of powers in matters of infringement and validity as provided for in the 1975 Luxembourg Convention.

In addition, the Conference succeeded in resolving the problems still posed by the draft Protocol on the Statute of the Common Appeal Court and by that on Privileges and Immunities.

As regards the third objective, that of the participation of Greece and the two acceding States in the system, it seemed so interwoven with the first objective that it was impossible to achieve it. The Conference proceedings, however, gave delegations a better understanding of these countries' problems and should contribute to a satisfactory solution to them in the near future.

In conclusion the Conference established the following texts:

- the Agreement relating to Community Patents,

- the Protocol conferring Powers in respect of Community Patents on certain Institutions of the European Communities and

- the Joint Declaration of the Representatives of the Governments of the Member States.

In initialling these texts, the Representatives of the Governments of the Member States of the EEC and of the acceding States established them with a view to signature, which will take place once a solution to a certain number of problems has been found. The Conference will be reconvened in Luxembourg for the signing of these instruments on the invitation of the President of the Council.

These texts are published by the Council of the European Communities pursuant to Article 21 paragraph 1 of the Rules of Procedure of the Conference.

Pursuant to paragraph 2 of the same Article, the acts of the Conference (including the preparatory documents, the Conference documents and the Conference reports) will be published after the final minutes have been drawn up.

CONTENTS

FINAL ACT	9
AGREEMENT RELATING TO COMMUNITY PATENTS	17
- Protocol on the Settlement of Litigation concerning the Infringement and Validity of Community Patents	37
- Protocol on Privileges and Immunities of the Common Appeal Court	71
- Protocol on the Statute of the Common Appeal Court	85
- Protocol on Amendments to the Community Patent Convention	99
- Convention for the European Patent for the Common Market and Implementing Regulations as amended by the Protocol on Amendments	113
PROTOCOL CONFERRING POWERS IN RESPECT OF COMMUNITY PATENTS ON CERTAIN INSTITUTIONS OF THE EUROPEAN COMMUNITIES	199
JOINT DECLARATION	205
- Declaration on the adjustment of national patent law	209
- Declaration on the operation of the Common Appeal Court during a transitional period	211
- Supplementary Decision to the Decision on preparations for the commencement of the activities of the special departments of the European Patent Office	213

FINAL ACT

FINAL ACT

THE REPRESENTATIVES OF THE GOVERNMENTS OF THE MEMBER STATES OF THE EUROPEAN ECONOMIC COMMUNITY AND OF THE ACCEDING STATES,

Assembled at Luxembourg on the eighteenth day of December in the year one thousand nine hundred and eighty-five on the occasion of the Luxembourg Conference on the Community patent,

CONSIDERING that a solution to the problem of the entry into force of the Agreement relating to Community patents is being sought by the Representatives of the Governments of the Member States meeting within the Council of the European Communities, and that a solution to the problem of the financial obligations and benefits resulting for their States from that Agreement is being sought by these Representatives meeting within the Community Patent Interim Committee,

HAVE PLACED on record the fact that they have drawn up the texts listed below and, by initialling them, have established them with a view to signature which will take place once a solution to the outstanding problems has been found by unanimity by the representatives of the Governments of the Member States meeting within the Council of the European Communities or within the Community Patent Interim Committee and following a resolution by unanimity of possible problems unforeseen at the date of the adoption of this Act which might arise out of the established texts of the provisions of the Agreement and the four Protocols thereto:

- Agreement relating to Community Patents (LUX/FINAL/1/85 + Annex);

- Protocol conferring Powers in respect of Community Patents on certain Institutions of the European Communities (LUX/FINAL/2/85);

- Joint Declaration of the Representatives of the Governments of the Member States (LUX/FINAL/3/85);

HAVE DECIDED that the Conference will be reconvened at Luxembourg for signature of the instruments on invitation by the President of the Council of the European Communities.

Til bekræftelse heraf har undertegnede repræsentanter underskrevet denne slutakt.

Zu Urkund dessen haben die unterzeichneten Vertreter ihre Unterschriften unter diese Schlussakte gesetzt.

Εις πίστωση των ανωτέρω οι υπογεγραμμένοι αντιπρόσωποι υπέγραψαν την παρούσα Τελική Πράξη.

In witness whereof, the undersigned Representatives have affixed their signatures below this Final Act.

En fe de lo cual, los representantes abajo firmantes han suscrito la presente Acta Final.

En foi de quoi, les représentants soussignés ont apposé leurs signatures au bas du présent Acte final.

Dá fhianú sin, chuir na hIonadaithe thíos-sínithe a lámh leis an Ionstraim Chríochnaitheach seo.

In fede di che, i rappresentanti sottoscritti hanno apposto le loro firme in calce al presente atto finale.

Ten blijke waarvan de ondergetekende vertegenwoordigers hun handtekening onder deze Slotakte hebben gesteld.

Em fé do que, os representantes abaixo assinados apuseram as suas assinaturas no fim da presente Acta Final.

Udfærdiget i Luxembourg, den attende december nitten hundrede og femogfirs

Geschehen zu Luxemburg am achtzehnten Dezember neunzehnhundertfünfundachtzig

Έγινε στο Λουξεμβούργο στις δεκαοχτώ Δεκεμβρίου χίλια εννιακόσια ογδόντα πέντε

Done at Luxembourg on the eighteenth day of December in the year one thousand nine hundred and eighty-five

Hecho en Luxemburgo, el diez y ocho de diciembre de mil novecientos ochenta y cinco

Fait à Luxembourg, le dix-huit décembre mil neuf cent quatre-vingt-cinq

Arna dhéanamh i Lucsamburg, an t-ochtú lá déag de mhí na Nollag, sa bhliain míle naoi gcéad ochtó a cúig.

Fatto a lussemburgo, addi' diciotto dicembre millenovecentottantacinque

Gedaan te Luxemburg, de achttiende december negentienhonderd vijfentachtig

Feito no Luxemburgo, aos dezoito de Dezembro de mil novecentos e oitenta e cinco

Pour le Gouvernement du Royaume de Belgique
Voor de Regering van het Koninkrijk België

[signature]

For regeringen for Kongeriget Danmark

[signature]

Für die Regierung der Bundesrepublik Deutschland

[signature]

Για την Κυβέρνηση της Ελληνικής Δημοκρατίας

[signature]

Por el Gobierno del Reino de España

[signature]

Pour le Gouvernement de la République française

[signature]

Thar ceann Rialtas na hÉireann

[signature]

Per il Governo della Repubblica italiana

[signature]

Pour le Gouvernement du Grand-Duché de Luxembourg

[signature]

Voor de Regering van het Koninkrijk der Nederlanden

[signature]

Pelo Governo da República Portuguesa

[signature]

For the Government of the United Kingdom of Great Britain and Northern Ireland

Victor Tarnofsky

AGREEMENT RELATING TO COMMUNITY PATENTS

PREAMBLE

THE HIGH CONTRACTING PARTIES to the Treaty establishing the European Economic Community,

DESIRING to give unitary and autonomous effect to European patents granted in respect of their territories under the Convention on the Grant of European Patents of 5 October 1973,

ANXIOUS to establish a Community patent system which contributes to the attainment of the objectives of the Treaty establishing the European Economic Community and in particular to the elimination within the Community of the distortion of competition which may result from the territorial aspect of national protection rights,

CONSIDERING that one of the fundamental objectives of the Treaty establishing the European Economic Community is the abolition of obstacles to the free movement of goods,

CONSIDERING that one of the most suitable means of ensuring that this objective will be achieved, as regards the free movement of goods protected by patents, is the creation of a Community patent system,

CONSIDERING that the creation of such a Community patent system is therefore inseparable from the attainment of the objectives of the Treaty and thus linked with the Community legal order,

CONSIDERING that it is necessary for these purposes for the High Contracting Parties to conclude an Agreement which constitutes a special agreement within the meaning of Article 142 of the Convention on the Grant of European Patents, a regional patent treaty within the meaning of Article 45 paragraph 1 of the Patent Cooperation Treaty of 19 June 1970, and a special agreement within the meaning of Article 19 of the Convention for the Protection of Industrial Property, signed in Paris on 20 March 1883 and last revised on 14 July 1967,

CONSIDERING that the achievement of a common market which offers conditions similar to those of a national market necessitates the creation of legal instruments which enable enterprises to adapt their production and distribution activities to European scales,

CONSIDERING that the problem of dealing effectively with actions relating to Community patents and the problems arising from the separation of jurisdiction created by the Community Patent Convention as signed at Luxembourg on 15 December 1975 in respect of infringement and validity of Community patents will best be solved by giving jurisdiction in actions for infringement of a Community patent to national courts of first instance designated as Community patent courts which can at the same time consider the validity of the patent in suit and, where necessary, amend or revoke it; and that an appeal to national courts of second instance designated as Community patent courts should lie from judgments of these courts,

CONSIDERING however that uniform application of the law on infringement and validity of Community patents requires the setting up of a Community patent appeal court common to the Contracting States (Common Appeal Court) to hear on appeal referrals on questions of infringement and validity from the Community patent courts of second instance,

CONSIDERING that the same requirement of uniform application of the law leads to conferral upon the Common Appeal Court of jurisdiction to decide on appeals from the Revocation Divisions and the Patent Administration Division of the European Patent Office, thus replacing the Revocation Boards provided for in the Community Patent Convention as signed on 15 December 1975,

CONSIDERING that it is essential that the application of this Agreement must not operate against the application of the provisions of the Treaty establishing the European Economic Community and that the Court of Justice of the European Communities must be able to ensure the uniformity of the Community legal order,

/CONVINCED that a gradual implementation of the Community patent system, characterised by the creation during a transitional period of a unitary patent with effects beyond national frontiers for a majority of the Member States, will permit inventors and enterprises to evaluate the advantages of the system vis-à-vis the national and European patent systems which will continue to be available to them,/[1]

/ANXIOUS to promote the completion of the internal market and the establishment of a European technological community by means of such a patent,/[1]

---
[1] The text in square brackets will be maintained in the event of the Agreement entering into force with fewer than twelve ratifications.

CONVINCED therefore that the conclusion of this Agreement is necessary to facilitate the achievement of the tasks of the European Economic Community,

HAVE DECIDED to conclude this Agreement and to this end have designated as their Plenipotentiaries:

HIS MAJESTY THE KING OF THE BELGIANS:

HER MAJESTY THE QUEEN OF DENMARK:

THE PRESIDENT OF THE FEDERAL REPUBLIC OF GERMANY:

THE PRESIDENT OF THE HELLENIC REPUBLIC:

HIS MAJESTY THE KING OF SPAIN:

THE PRESIDENT OF THE FRENCH REPUBLIC:

THE PRESIDENT OF IRELAND:

THE PRESIDENT OF THE ITALIAN REPUBLIC:

HIS ROYAL HIGHNESS THE GRAND DUKE OF LUXEMBOURG:

HER MAJESTY THE QUEEN OF THE NETHERLANDS:

THE PRESIDENT OF THE PORTUGUESE REPUBLIC:

HER MAJESTY THE QUEEN OF THE UNITED KINGDOM OF GREAT BRITAIN AND NORTHERN IRELAND:

WHO, meeting in the Council of the European Communities, having exchanged their full powers, found in good and due form,

HAVE AGREED AS FOLLOWS:

Article 1
Contents of the Agreement

1. The Convention for the European patent for the common market signed at Luxembourg on 15 December 1975, hereinafter referred to as "the Community Patent Convention", shall be amended and supplemented by the following Protocols which are annexed to this Agreement:

- Protocol on the Settlement of Litigation concerning the Infringement and Validity of Community Patents, hereinafter referred to as "the Protocol on Litigation",

- Protocol on Privileges and Immunities of the Common Appeal Court,

- Protocol on the Statute of the Common Appeal Court,

- Protocol on Amendments to the Community Patent Convention, hereinafter referred to as "the Protocol on Amendments".

2. The Community Patent Convention, as amended by the Protocol on Amendments, is annexed to this Agreement.

3. The Annexes to this Agreement shall form an integral part thereof.

4. On entry into force of this Agreement, it shall replace the Community Patent Convention in the form signed at Luxembourg on 15 December 1975.

Article 2
Relationship with the Community legal order

1. No provision of this Agreement may be invoked against the application of the Treaty establishing the European Economic Community.

2. In order to ensure the uniformity of the Community legal order, the Common Appeal Court established by the Protocol on Litigation shall request the Court of Justice of the European Communities to give a preliminary ruling in accordance with Article 177 of the Treaty establishing the European Economic Community whenever there is a risk of an interpretation of this Agreement being inconsistent with that Treaty.

3. Where a Member State or the Commission of the European Communities considers that a decision of the Common Appeal Court which closes the procedure before it does not comply with the principle stated in the foregoing paragraphs, it may request the Court of Justice of the European Communities to give a ruling. The ruling given by the Court of Justice in response to such request shall not affect the decision by the Common Appeal Court which gave rise to the request. The Registrar of the Court of Justice shall give notice of the request to the Member States, to the Council and, if the request is made by a Member State, the Commission of the European Communities; they shall then be entitled within two months of the notification to submit statements of case or written observations to the Court. No fees shall be levied or any costs or expenses awarded in respect of the proceedings provided for in this paragraph.

Article 3
Interpretation of provisions on jurisdiction

1. The Court of Justice of the European Communities shall have jurisdiction to give preliminary rulings concerning the interpretation of the provisions on jurisdiction applicable to actions relating to Community patents brought before national courts, contained in Part VI, Chapter I, of the Community Patent Convention and in the Protocol on Litigation.

2. The following courts shall have the power to request the Court of Justice to give a preliminary ruling on any question of interpretation as defined in paragraph 1:

(a) - in Belgium: la Cour de cassation (het Hof van Cassatie) and le Conseil d'Etat (de Raad van State),

- in Denmark: Højesteret,

- in the Federal Republic of Germany: die obersten Gerichtshöfe des Bundes,

- in Greece: τα ανώτατα Δικαστήρια,

- in Spain: el Tribunal Supremo

- in France: la Cour de cassation and le Conseil d'Etat,

- in Ireland: an Chúirt Uachtarach (the Supreme Court),

- in Italy: la Corte suprema di cassazione,

- in Luxembourg: la Cour supérieure de justice when sitting as Cour de cassation,

- in the Netherlands: de Hoge Raad,

- in Portugal: o Supremo Tribunal de Justiça

- in the United Kingdom: the House of Lords.

Article 3 (continued)

(b) the courts of the Contracting States when ruling on appeals.

3. Where such a question is raised in a case before one of the courts listed in paragraph 2(a), that court must, if it considers that a decision on the question is necessary to enable it to give a judgment, request the Court of Justice to give a ruling thereon.

4. Where such a question is raised before one of the courts referred to in paragraph 2(b), that court may, under the conditions laid down in paragraph 1, request the Court of Justice to give a ruling thereon.

Article 4
Rules of Procedure of the Court of Justice

1. The Protocol on the Statute of the Court of Justice of the European Economic Community and the Rules of Procedure of the Court of Justice shall apply to any proceedings referred to in Articles 2 and 3.

2. The Rules of Procedure shall be adapted and supplemented, as necessary, in conformity with Article 188 of the Treaty establishing the European Economic Community.

Article 5
Jurisdiction of the Common Appeal Court

Subject to Articles 2 and 3, the Common Appeal Court shall ensure uniform interpretation and application of this Agreement and of the provisions enacted in implementation thereof, to the extent to which these are not national provisions.

Article 6
Ratification

This Agreement shall be subject to ratification by the signatory States. Instruments of ratification shall be deposited with the Secretary-General of the Council of the European Communities.

Article 7
Accession

1. This Agreement shall be open to accession by States becoming Member States of the European Economic Community.

2. Instruments of accession to this Agreement shall be deposited with the Secretary-General of the Council of the European Communities. Accession shall take effect on the first day of the third month following the deposit of the instrument of accession, provided that the ratification by the State concerned of the Convention on the Grant of European Patents, hereinafter referred to as "the European Patent Convention", or its accession thereto has become effective.

3. The signatory States hereby recognise that any State which becomes a member of the European Economic Community must accede to this Agreement.

4. A special agreement may be concluded between the Contracting States and the acceding State to determine the details of application of this Agreement necessitated by the accession of that State.

Article 8
Participation of third States

The Council of the European Communities may, acting by a unanimous decision, invite a State party to the European Patent Convention which forms a customs union or a free trade area with the European Economic Community to enter into negotiations with a view to enabling that third State to participate in this Agreement on the basis of a special agreement, to be concluded between the Contracting States to this Agreement and the third State concerned, determining the conditions and details for applying this Agreement to that State.

Article 9
Territorial field of application

1. This Agreement shall apply to the European territories of the Contracting States and, as far as the Kingdom of Spain and the French Republic are concerned, to their entire territories.

2. Notwithstanding paragraph 1:

(a) this Agreement shall apply neither to the Faroe Islands nor to Greenland, unless the Kingdom of Denmark makes a declaration to the contrary;

(b) this Agreement shall not apply to any European territory situated outside the United Kingdom of Great Britain and Northern Ireland for the international relations of which the United Kingdom is responsible, unless the United Kingdom makes a declaration to the contrary in respect of any such territory;

(c) this Agreement shall apply to the Netherlands Antilles and Aruba, if the Kingdom of the Netherlands makes a declaration to that effect.

Article 9 (continued)

3. Such declarations may be made in the instrument of ratification of the State concerned or by notification addressed to the Secretary-General of the Council of the European Communities at any later time.

4. If such a declaration is contained in the instrument of ratification, it shall take effect on the same date as the ratification; if the declaration is made in a notification after the deposit of the instrument of ratification, it shall take effect six months after the date of receipt by the Secretary-General of the Council of the European Communities.

5. The States referred to in paragraph 2(b) and (c) may, at any time, declare that the Agreement shall cease to apply to one or more of their territories in respect of which they have made a declaration pursuant to paragraph 2(b) or (c). Such declarations of termination shall take effect one year after the date on which the Secretary-General of the Council of the European Communities received notification thereof.

6. This Agreement shall also apply to the sea and submarine areas adjacent to a territory to which the Agreement applies by virtue of the preceding paragraphs in which one of the Contracting States excercises sovereign rights or jurisdiction in accordance with international law.

Article 10
Entry into force

1. In order to enter into force, this Agreement must be ratified by ... States whose ratification of the European Patent Convention or accession thereto has become effective. This Agreement shall enter into force on the first day of the third month following the deposit of the last instrument of ratification by such a State. /However, if the Protocol conferring Powers in respect of Community Patents on certain Institutions of the European Communities enters into force at a later date, this Agreement shall enter into force on the date of entry into force of that Protocol./[2]

/2. Any ratification after the entry into force of this Agreement shall take effect on the first day of the third month following the deposit of the instrument of ratification, provided that the ratification by the State concerned of the European Patent Convention or its accession thereto has become effective./[2]

Article 11
Observers

As long as this Agreement has not entered into force in respect of a Member State of the European Economic Community, that State may take part as an observer in the Select Committee of the Administrative Council of the European Patent Organisation, hereinafter referred to as "the Select Committee" and in the Administrative Committee of the Common Appeal Court, hereinafter referred to as "the Administrative Committee", and may appoint a representative and an alternate representative to each of these bodies for this purpose.

---

[2] The text in square brackets will be maintained in the event of the Agreement entering into force with fewer than twelve ratifications.

/Article 12

Application of the Agreement in the case of later ratification

Any signatory State which ratifies this Agreement after its entry into force may submit to the Select Committee for approval the technical details of application of this Agreement with respect to it./[3]

Article 13
Duration of the Agreement

This Agreement is concluded for an unlimited period.

Article 14
Revision

If a majority of the Member States of the European Economic Community requests the revision of this Agreement, a revision conference shall be convened by the President of the Council of the European Communities. The conference shall be prepared by the Select Committee or by the Administrative Committee, each acting within the limits of its own competence.

---

[3] The text in square brackets will be maintained in the event of the Agreement entering into force with fewer than twelve ratifications.

Article 15
Disputes between Contracting States

1.   Any dispute between Contracting States concerning the interpretation or application of this Agreement which is not settled by negotiation shall be submitted, at the request of one of the States concerned, to the Select Committee or to the Administrative Committee as the case may be. The body to which the dispute is submitted shall endeavour to bring about agreement between the States concerned.

2.   If agreement is not reached within six months from the date when the Select Committee or the Administrative Committee was seised of the dispute, any one of the States concerned may submit the dispute to the Court of Justice of the European Communities.

3.   If the Court of Justice finds that a Contracting State has failed to fulfil an obligation under this Agreement, that State shall be required to take the necessary measures to comply with the judgment of the Court of Justice.

Article 16
Definition

For the purposes of this Agreement "Contracting State" means a State for which the Agreement is in force.

Article 17
Original of the Agreement

This Agreement, drawn up in a single original in the Danish, Dutch, English, French, German, Greek, Irish, Italian, Portuguese and Spanish languages, all ten texts being equally authentic, shall be deposited in the archives of the General Secretariat of the Council of the European Communities. The Secretary-General shall transmit a certified copy to the Government of each Member State of the European Economic Community.

Article 18
Notification

The Secretary-General of the Council of the European Communities shall notify the Member States of the European Economic Community of:

(a) the deposit of each instrument of ratification and accession;

(b) the date of entry into force of this Agreement;

(c) any declaration or notification received pursuant to Article 9 of this Agreement;

(d) any reservation or withdrawal of reservation pursuant to Article 88 or 89 of the Community Patent Convention;

(e) any notification received pursuant to Article 1 paragraphs 2 and 3 of the Protocol on Litigation.

In witness whereof, the undersigned Plenipotentiaries have affixed their signatures below this Agreement.

Done at .... on ....

PROTOCOL
ON THE SETTLEMENT OF LITIGATION
CONCERNING THE INFRINGEMENT AND VALIDITY
OF COMMUNITY PATENTS

(Protocol on Litigation)

PART I
GENERAL PROVISIONS

Article 1
Community patent courts

1. The Contracting States shall designate in their territories as limited a number as possible of national courts and tribunals of first and second instance, hereinafter referred to as "Community patent courts", which shall perform the functions assigned to them by this Protocol.

2. The names of the Community patent courts and their territorial jurisdiction are specified in the Annex to this Protocol. However, as regards the Kingdom of Spain and the Portuguese Republic, the names of these courts and their territorial jurisdiction shall be notified to the Secretary-General of the Council of the European Communities at the latest at the time of ratification of the Agreement relating to Community Patents.

3. Any change in the number, the names or territorial jurisdiction of the courts shall be notified by the Contracting State concerned to the Secretary-General of the Council of the European Communities.

Article 2
Common Appeal Court

1. A Community patent appeal court, common to the Contracting States, hereinafter referred to as "the Common Appeal Court", shall be established by the present Protocol. The Common Appeal Court shall perform the functions assigned to it by this Protocol.

2. The seat of the Common Appeal Court shall be determined by common accord of the Governments of the signatory States.

Article 3
Legal status

1. The Common Appeal Court shall have legal personality.

2. In each of the Contracting States, the Common Appeal Court shall enjoy the most extensive legal capacity accorded to legal persons under the national law of that State; it may in particular acquire or dispose of movable and immovable property and may be a party to legal proceedings.

3. The President of the Common Appeal Court shall represent the Common Appeal Court.

Article 4
Privileges and immunities

The Protocol on Privileges and Immunities of the Common Appeal Court shall define the conditions under which the Common Appeal Court, its judges, the members of the Administrative Committee, the officials and other servants of the Common Appeal Court and such other persons specified in that Protocol as take part in the work of the Common Appeal Court shall enjoy, in the territory of each Contracting State, the privileges and immunities necessary for the performance of their duties.

Article 5
Plenum and registry

1. The Common Appeal Court shall be constituted by the necessary number of judges to be determined by the Administrative Committee, acting unanimously, after consulting the Common Appeal Court; this number shall be at least equal to the number of Contracting States.

2. The Common Appeal Court shall sit in plenary session. It may however form chambers, each consisting of the number of judges set out in its Rules of Procedure.

3. The Common Appeal Court shall have a registry.

Article 6
Appointment of the judges of the Common Appeal Court

1. The judges of the Common Appeal Court shall be chosen from persons who possess the qualifications required for appointment to judicial office in their respective State and experience in patent law; they shall be appointed by common accord of the representatives of the Governments of the Contracting States, for a term of six years.

2. Retiring judges shall be eligible for reappointment.

Article 7
President of the Common Appeal Court

1. The judges shall elect the President of the Common Appeal Court from among their number for a term of three years. He may be re-elected.

2. If the President is absent or indisposed, another member of the Court shall take his place, in order of seniority.

Article 8
Management

The Common Appeal Court shall be managed by its President. For the administration of the Common Appeal Court, its financial management and its accounts, the President shall be responsible to the Administrative Committee.

Article 9
Administrative Committee

1. The Administrative Committee shall be composed of the representatives of the Contracting States, the representative of the Commission of the European Communities and their alternate representatives. Each Contracting State and the Commission shall be entitled to appoint one representative and one alternate representative to the Administrative Committee. Where appropriate, the President of the Common Appeal Court shall take part in the deliberations of the Administrative Committee.

2. Article 15 paragraph 2, Article 16, Article 17, Article 18 paragraphs 1, 3, 4 and 5, Article 20 paragraph 2, Article 21, Article 22 and Article 23 of the Community Patent Convention shall apply mutatis mutandis to the Administrative Committee.

Article 10
Cover of expenditure

1. Expenditure of the Common Appeal Court shall be covered:

   (a) by the Common Appeal Court's own resources;

   (b) by financial contributions from the Contracting States, the amount of which shall be determined / .... /[4]

2. Each Contracting State may ask the European Patent Office to pay to the Common Appeal Court the contribution which that State is bound to make pursuant to paragraph 1(b) by drawing from the revenue due to that State pursuant to Article 24 /paragraph 2/[4] of the Community Patent Convention.

/3. The provisions laid down in paragraph 1 shall also be included in the examination of the system of financing for the special departments of the European Patent Office provided for in Article 24 paragraph 3 of the Community Patent Convention. When this examination has been concluded this Article may also be amended by a unanimous decision of the Council of the European Communities acting on a proposal by the Commission./[4]

---

[4] The contents of the square brackets are to be decided later following examination of Article 24 of the Community Patent Convention by the Community Patent Interim Committee.

Article 10 (continued)

4. Articles 42 to 48 of the European Patent Convention shall apply to the Common Appeal Court, the Administrative Committee acting in place of the Administrative Council of the European Patent Organisation and the President of the Common Appeal Court acting in place of the President of the European Patent Office.

5. The income and expenditure account and a balance sheet of the Common Appeal Court shall be examined by the Court of Auditors of the European Communities. The audit, which shall be based on vouchers and shall take place, if necessary, on the spot, shall ascertain that all income has been received and all expenditure effected in a lawful and proper manner and that the financial management is sound. The Court of Auditors shall draw up a report after the end of each accounting period.

6. The President of the Common Appeal Court shall annually submit to the Administrative Committee the accounts of the preceding accounting period in respect of the budget and the balance sheet showing the assets and liabilities of the Common Appeal Court together with the report of the Court of Auditors.

7. The Administrative Committee shall approve the annual accounts together with the report of the Court of Auditors and shall give the President of the Common Appeal Court a discharge in respect of the implementation of the budget.

Article 11
Remuneration of the members of the
Common Appeal Court and Staff Regulations

1. The Administrative Committee shall determine the salaries, allowances and pensions of the President and judges of the Common Appeal Court. It shall also determine any payment to be made instead of remuneration.

2. The Administrative Committee shall lay down the Staff Regulations of the officials of the Common Appeal Court and the Conditions of Employment of other servants of the Common Appeal Court.

3. A majority of three-quarters of the votes of the Contracting States represented and voting shall be required for the decisions which the Administrative Committee is empowered to take under this Article. Abstentions shall not be considered as votes.

Article 12
Rules of Procedure
of the Common Appeal Court

The Common Appeal Court shall adopt its Rules of Procedure which shall, _inter alia_, lay down the language arrangements of the Court. The Rules of Procedure shall be subject to the unanimous approval of the Administrative Committee.

PART II
PROVISIONS ON INTERNATIONAL JURISDICTION AND ENFORCEMENT

Article 13
Application of the Convention on Jurisdiction and Enforcement

1. Unless otherwise specified in this Protocol, the Convention on Jurisdiction and the Enforcement of Judgments in Civil and Commercial Matters, signed in Brussels on 27 September 1968, as amended by the Conventions on the Accession to that Convention of the States acceding to the European Communities, the whole of which Convention and of which Conventions of Accession are hereinafter referred to as "the Convention on Jurisdiction and Enforcement", shall apply to proceedings governed by this Protocol.

2. Article 2, Article 4, Article 5 paragraphs 1, 3, 4 and 5, and Article 24 of the Convention on Jurisdiction and Enforcement shall not apply to proceedings governed by this Protocol. Articles 17 and 18 of that Convention shall apply subject to the limitations in Article 14 paragraph 4 of this Protocol.

3. For the purpose of applying the Convention on Jurisdiction and Enforcement to proceedings governed by this Protocol, the provisions of Title II of that Convention which are applicable to persons domiciled in a Contracting State shall also be applicable to persons who do not have a domicile in any Contracting State but have an establishment therein.

Article 14
Jurisdiction

1. Subject to the provisions of this Protocol as well as to any provisions of the Convention on Jurisdiction and Enforcement applicable by virtue of Article 13, proceedings governed by this Protocol shall be brought in the courts of the Contracting State in which the defendant is domiciled or, if he is not domiciled in any of the Contracting States, in which he has an establishment.

2. If the defendant neither is domiciled nor has an establishment in any of the Contracting States, such proceedings shall be brought in the courts of the Contracting State in which the plaintiff is domiciled or, if he is not domiciled in any of the Contracting States, in which he has an establishment.

3. If neither the defendant nor the plaintiff is so domiciled or has such an establishment, such proceedings shall be brought in the courts of the Contracting State where the Common Appeal Court has its seat.

4. Notwithstanding the provisions of paragraphs 1 to 3 above:

(a) Article 17 of the Convention on Jurisdiction and Enforcement shall apply if the parties agree that a different Community patent court shall have jurisdiction;

(b) Article 18 of that Convention shall apply if the defendant enters an appearance before a different Community patent court.

5. The proceedings governed by this Protocol, with the exception of actions for a declaration of non-infringement of a Community patent, may also be brought in the courts of the Contracting State in which the act of infringement has been committed or threatened, or in which an act within the meaning of Article 15 paragraph 1(c) has been committed.

PART III
FIRST INSTANCE

Article 15
Jurisdiction over infringement and validity

1. The Community patent courts of first instance shall have exclusive jurisdiction:

(a) for all infringement actions and - if they are permitted under national law - actions in respect of threatened infringement relating to Community patents;

(b) for actions for a declaration of non-infringement, if they are permitted under national law;

(c) for all actions in respect of the use made of the invention during the period specified in Article 34 paragraph 1 of the Community Patent Convention;

(d) for counterclaims for revocation of the Community patent pursuant to paragraph 2.

2. The Community patent courts of first instance shall treat the Community patent as valid unless its validity is put in issue by the defendant with a counterclaim for revocation of the Community patent. The counterclaim may only be based on the grounds for revocation mentioned in Article 57 paragraph 1 of the Community Patent Convention. The second phrase of Article 56 paragraph 1 and Article 56 paragraphs 2,3 and 6 of the Community Patent Convention shall apply.

Article 15 (continued)

3. If the counterclaim is brought in a legal action to which the proprietor of the patent is not already a party, he shall be informed thereof and may be joined as a party to the action in accordance with the conditions set out in national law.

4. The validity of a Community patent may not be put in issue in an action for a declaration of non-infringement.

Article 16
Information to the European Patent Office

The Community patent court of first instance with which a counterclaim for revocation of the Community patent has been filed shall inform the European Patent Office of the date on which the counterclaim for revocation was filed. The latter shall record this fact in the Register of Community Patents.

Article 17
Territorial jurisdiction

1. A Community patent court of first instance whose jurisdiction is based on Article 14 paragraphs 1 to 4 shall have jurisdiction in respect of

- acts of infringement committed or threatened within the territory of any of the Contracting States;

- acts within the meaning of Article 15 paragraph 1(c) committed within the territory of any of the Contracting States.

2. A Community patent court of first instance whose jurisdiction is based on Article 14 paragraph 5 shall have jurisdiction only in respect of acts committed or threatened within the territory of the State in which that court is situated.

Article 18
Stay of proceedings

If the judgment in an action before a Community patent court of first instance relating to a European patent application which may result in the grant of a Community patent depends upon the patentability of the invention, that judgment may be given only after the European Patent Office has granted a Community patent or refused the European patent application.

Article 19
Judgments on validity

1. Where, in a proceeding before the Community patent courts of first instance, the validity of a Community patent has been put in issue,

   (a) if any of the grounds for revocation mentioned in Article 57 paragraph 1 of the Community Patent Convention are found to prejudice the maintenance of the Community patent, the court shall order the revocation of the patent;

   (b) if none of the grounds for revocation mentioned in Article 57 paragraph 1 of the Community Patent Convention is found to prejudice the maintenance of the Community patent, the court shall reject the application for revocation;

Article 19 (continued)

(c) if, taking into consideration the amendments made by the proprietor of the patent during the course of the action, none of the grounds for revocation mentioned in Article 57 paragraph 1 of the Community Patent Convention are found to prejudice the maintenance of the Community patent, the court shall order the patent to be maintained as amended.

2. Where a Community patent court of first instance has given a judgment which has become final on a counterclaim for revocation of the Community patent, it shall send a copy of the judgment to the European Patent Office. Any party may request information about such transmission.

3. Where a Community patent court of first instance, by a judgment which has become final, has decided to maintain the Community patent as amended, it shall send a copy of the judgment to the European Patent Office with the text of the patent as amended as a result of the proceedings. Any party may request information about such transmission. The European Patent Office shall publish the text provided that:

(a) a translation of any amended claims in one of the official languages of each of the Contracting States which does not have as an official language the language of the proceedings of the court is filed within a time limit identical to that referred to in Article 59 paragraph 3(b) of the Community Patent Convention;

(b) the fee for the printing of a new specification is paid within a time limit identical to that referred to in Article 59 paragraph 3(c) of the Community Patent Convention.

Article 19 (continued)

4. If a translation is not filed in due time or if the fee for the printing of a new specification is not paid in due time, the European Patent Office shall, notwithstanding the decision of the Community patent court, revoke the Community patent unless these acts are done and the additional fee is paid within a further period identical to that referred to in Article 59 paragraph 4 of the Community Patent Convention.

Article 20
Effect of judgments on validity

When it has become final, a judgment of a Community patent court of first instance revoking or amending a Community patent shall have, subject to Article 57 paragraph 3 of the Community Patent Convention, in all Contracting States the effects specified in Article 35 of that Convention.

PART IV
SECOND INSTANCE

Article 21
Jurisdiction of the Community patent courts of second instance

1. An appeal to the Community patent courts of second instance shall lie from judgments of the Community patent courts of first instance in respect of proceedings referred to in Article 15 paragraph 1.

2. The conditions under which an appeal may be lodged with a Community patent court of second instance shall be determined by the national law of the Contracting State in which that court is located.

Article 22
Jurisdiction of the Common Appeal Court in respect of issues raised on appeal before Community patent courts of second instance

The Common Appeal Court shall have exclusive jurisdiction to determine issues raised on appeal before the Community patent courts of second instance concerning:

(a) the effects of the Community patent and the European patent application as provided in Articles 29 to 35 inclusive of the Community Patent Convention, insofar as questions of national law are not involved;

(b) the validity of the Community patent put in issue pursuant to Article 15 paragraph 2.

Article 23
Referrals from the Community patent courts of second instance to the Common Appeal Court

1. Where an appeal to a Community patent court of second instance raises issues in respect of which the Common Appeal Court has exclusive jurisdiction pursuant to Article 22, the court of second instance shall stay its proceedings insofar as they require a judgment on such issues and refer them to the Common Appeal Court for a judgment. A decision to stay proceedings and refer any of the issues mentioned in Article 22 to the Common Appeal Court may be taken without oral proceedings taking place.

2. However, the Community patent court of second instance may continue its proceedings provided that there is no possibility of the judgment of the Common Appeal Court being prejudged.

3. The Community patent court of second instance may not render a final judgment before the judgment of the Common Appeal Court has been given.

Article 24
Nature of proceedings before the Common Appeal Court

The Common Appeal Court shall examine all the issues of which it is seised and give a ruling on fact and law.

Article 25
Judgments of the Common Appeal Court

1. Where a judgment is given by the Common Appeal Court on an issue referred to in Article 22(a) it shall find whether the Community patent or the European patent application has or has not the effects at issue.

2. Where a judgment is given by the Common Appeal Court on an issue referred to in Article 22(b), Articles 19 and 20 shall apply mutatis mutandis.

Article 26
Applicable law

The Common Appeal Court shall apply the provisions of the Agreement relating to Community patents.

Article 27
Effect of the judgment

A judgment given by the Common Appeal Court shall be binding in the further proceedings of the case.

Article 28

Supplementary jurisdiction of the Common Appeal Court

1. The Common Appeal Court shall decide on appeals from decisions of the Revocation Divisions and the Patent Administration Division of the European Patent Office.

2. If proceedings in respect of a Community patent are pending before it, the Common Appeal Court shall, if necessary, decide on the lapse of that patent.

3. Where the Common Appeal Court has given a judgment pursuant to paragraph 1 or 2 it shall send a copy of the judgment to the European Patent Office. Any party may request information about such transmission.

PART V
THIRD INSTANCE AND PRELIMINARY RULING PROCEDURE

Article 29

Further appeal to national courts

The national rules concerning further appeal shall be applicable in respect of judgments of Community patent courts of second instance on matters upon which the Common Appeal Court does not have exclusive jurisdiction under Article 22.

Article 30
Preliminary ruling procedure before the Common Appeal Court

1. The Common Appeal Court shall have, in accordance with Article 5 of the Agreement relating to Community Patents, jurisdiction to give preliminary rulings concerning:

(a) the interpretation of the Agreement in respect of matters not falling within its exclusive jurisdiction as provided in Article 22 of this Protocol;

(b) the validity and interpretation of provisions enacted in implementation of the Agreement, to the extent to which they are not national provisions.

2. Where such a question is raised before a national court, that court may, if it considers that a decision on the question is necessary to enable it to give judgment, request the Common Appeal Court to give a ruling thereon.

3. Where any such question is raised in a case pending before a national court against whose decisions there is no judicial remedy under national law, that court shall bring the matter before the Common Appeal Court.

4. The term "courts" shall include the authorities referred to in Article 72 of the Community Patent Convention.

PART VI
COMMON PROVISIONS FOR THE COMMUNITY PATENT COURTS OF FIRST AND SECOND INSTANCE

Article 31
Qualifications of judges

The judges of the Community patent courts shall be persons who possess experience of patent law.

Article 32
Applicable law

1. The Community patent courts shall apply the provisions of the Agreement relating to Community Patents.

2. On all matters not covered by the Agreement relating to Community Patents a Community patent court shall apply its national law, including its private international law.

Article 33
Procedure

1. Unless otherwise specified in the Agreement relating to Community Patents, a Community patent court shall apply the rules of procedure governing the same type of action relating to a national patent in the Contracting State where it has its seat.

2. Paragraph 1 shall apply *mutatis mutandis* in the case of a European patent application which may result in the grant of a Community patent.

3. The Community patent court shall record in writing at least the essentials of the oral proceedings, including the testimony given and the summary examination of the items produced in evidence; it shall attach the procedural acts and written statements.

Article 34
Specific rules on related actions

1. A Community patent court hearing an action referred to in Article 15 paragraph 1, other than an action for a declaration of non-infringement, shall, unless there are special grounds for continuing the hearing, at the request of one of the parties and after hearing the other parties, stay the proceedings where the validity of the Community patent is already in issue before another Community patent court or before the Common Appeal Court, or where opposition to the Community patent has already been lodged or an application for revocation or a request for limitation of the Community patent has been filed at the European Patent Office.

2. The European Patent Office, when hearing an application for revocation or a request for limitation of a Community patent shall, unless there are special grounds for continuing the hearing, at the request of one of the parties and after hearing the other parties, stay the proceedings where the validity of the Community patent is already in issue before a Community patent court or before the Common Appeal Court.

Article 35
Sanctions

1. Where a Community patent court finds that the defendant has infringed or threatened to infringe a Community patent, it shall, unless there are special reasons for not doing so, issue an order prohibiting the defendant from proceeding with the acts which infringed or would infringe the Community patent. It shall also take such measures in accordance with its national law as are aimed at ensuring that this prohibition is complied with.

2. In all other respects the Community patent court shall apply the law of the Contracting State in which the acts of infringement or threatened infringement were committed.

Article 36
Provisional, including protective, measures

1. Application may be made to the courts of a Contracting State, including Community patent courts, for such provisional, including protective, measures in respect of a Community patent as may be available under the law of that State in respect of a national patent, even if, under this Protocol, a Community patent court of another Contracting State has jurisdiction as to the substance of the matter.

2. A Community patent court whose jurisdiction is based on Article 14 paragraphs 1, 2, 3, or 4 shall have jurisdiction to grant provisional, including protective, measures which, subject to any necessary procedure for recognition and enforcement pursuant to Title III of the Convention on Jurisdiction and Enforcement, are applicable in the territory of any Contracting State. No other court shall have such jurisdiction.

3. The Common Appeal Court shall not be competent to order provisional, including protective, measures and no appeal may be made to the Common Appeal Court against a judgment ordering such measures.

PART VII
TRANSITIONAL PROVISIONS

Article 37
Proceedings to which the Protocol applies

This Protocol shall only apply to proceedings initiated after the entry into force of the Agreement relating to Community Patents.

Article 38
Application of the Convention on Jurisdiction and Enforcement

The provisions of the Convention on Jurisdiction and Enforcement rendered applicable by the preceding Articles shall not have effect in respect of any Contracting State for which that Convention has not yet entered into force until such entry into force.

Article 39
Appointment of judges to the Common Appeal Court during a transitional period

1. During a transitional period, the expiry of which shall be determined by the Administrative Committee, that Committee may, in accordance with the conditions set out in Article 5 paragraph 1, determine a number of judges of the Common Appeal Court which is smaller than the number of Contracting States.

2. During the transitional period referred to in paragraph 1, the representatives of the Governments of the Contracting States may appoint as judges of the Common Appeal Court persons who possess the qualifications required for appointment to judicial office in their respective States and experience in patent law. The judges may continue their activities in their respective States or in international organizations. They may be appointed for a term of less than six years, though this shall not be less than one year. They may be reappointed.

ANNEX

COMMUNITY PATENT COURTS

Contracting State	Name of the Court (a) First instance (b) Second instance	Territorial jurisdiction
BELGIQUE	a) Tribunal de première instance de Bruxelles b) Cour d'Appel de Bruxelles	Toute la Belgique Toute la Belgique
BELGIE	a) Rechtbank van eerste aanleg Brussel b) Hof van Beroep te Brussel	Hele Belgische grondgebied Hele Belgische grondgebied
DANMARK	a) - Østre landsret - Vestre landsret b) Højesteret	Staden København og øernes amter Jyllands amter Hele riget
DEUTSCHLAND	a) - Landgericht Braunschweig - Landgericht Düsseldorf - Landgericht Frankfurt (Main) - Landgericht Hamburg - Landgericht Mannheim - Landgericht München I - Landgericht Nürnberg-Fürth - Landgericht Berlin - Landgericht Saarbrücken b) - Oberlandesgericht Braunschweig - Oberlandesgericht Düsseldorf - Oberlandesgericht Frankfurt (Main) - Oberlandesgericht Hamburg - Oberlandesgericht Karlsruhe - Oberlandesgericht München - Oberlandesgericht Nürnberg - Kammergericht Berlin - Oberlandesgericht Saarbrücken	- Land Niedersachsen - Land Nordrhein-Westfalen - Länder Hessen und Rheinland-Pfalz - Länder Bremen, Hamburg und Schleswig-Holstein - Land Baden-Württemberg - Oberlandesgerichtsbezirk München - Oberlandesgerichtsbezirke Nürnberg und Bamberg - Land Berlin - Saarland - Land Niedersachsen - Land Nordrhein-Westfalen - Länder Hessen und Rheinland-Pfalz - Länder Bremen, Hamburg und Schleswig-Holstein - Land Baden-Württemberg - Oberlandesgerichtsbezirk München - Oberlandesgerichtsbezirke Nürnberg und Bamberg - Land Berlin - Saarland

Contracting State	Name of the Court (a) First instance (b) Second instance	Territorial jurisdiction
ΕΛΛΑΔΑ	a) - Πρωτοδικείο Αθηνών	- Περιφέρειες των Εφετείων Αθηνών, Πειραιώς, Πατρών, Ναυπλίου, Κρήτης και Δωδεκανήσου
	- Πρωτοδικείο Θεσσαλονίκης	- Περιφέρειες των Εφετείων Θεσσαλονίκης, Θράκης, Αιγαίου, Λαρίσσης, Ιωαννίνων και Κερκύρας
	β) - Εφετείο Αθηνών	- Περιφέρειες των Εφετείων Αθηνών, Πειραιώς, Πατρών, Ναυπλίου, Κρήτης και Δωδεκανήσου
	- Εφετείο Θεσσαλονίκης	- Περιφέρειες των Εφετείων Θεσσαλονίκης, Θράκης, Αιγαίου, Λαρίσσης, Ιωαννίνων και Κερκύρας
FRANCE		Les ressorts des Cours d'appel de :
	a) - Tribunal de Marseille	- Aix-en-Provence, Bastia, Nîmes
	- Tribunal de Bordeaux	- Agen, Bordeaux, Poitiers
	- Tribunal de Strasbourg	- Colmar
	- Tribunal de Lille	- Amiens, Douai
	- Tribunal de Limoges	- Bourges, Limoges, Riom
	- Tribunal de Lyon	- Chambéry, Lyon, Grenoble
	- Tribunal de Nancy	- Besançon, Dijon, Nancy
	- Tribunal de Paris	- Orléans, Paris, Versailles, Reims, Rouen, Basse Terre, Fort-de-France, Saint-Denis (Réunion), Nouméa, Papeete
	- Tribunal de Rennes	- Angers, Caen, Rennes
	- Tribunal de Toulouse	- Pau, Montpellier, Toulouse

Contracting State	Name of the Court (a) First instance (b) Second instance	Territorial jurisdiction
FRANCE		Les ressorts des Cours d'appel de :
	b) - Cour d'appel d'Aix	- Aix-en-Provence, Bastia, Nîmes
	- Cour d'appel de Bordeaux	- Agen, Bordeaux, Poitiers
	- Cour d'appel de Colmar	- Colmar
	- Cour d'appel de Douai	- Amiens, Douai
	- Cour d'appel de Limoges	- Bourges, Limoges, Riom
	- Cour d'appel de Lyon	- Chambéry, Lyon, Grenoble
	- Cour d'appel de Nancy	- Besançon, Dijon, Nancy
	- Cour d'appel de Paris	- Orléans, Paris, Versailles, Reims, Rouen, Basse Terre, Fort-de-France, Saint-Denis (Réunion), Nouméa, Papeete
	- Cour d'appel de Rennes	- Angers, Caen, Rennes
	- Cour d'appel de Toulouse	- Pau, Montpellier, Toulouse
EIRE	a) An Ard-Chúirt	Éire go huile
	b) An Chúirt Uachtarach	Éire go huile
IRELAND	a) The High Court	All of Ireland
	b) The Supreme Court	All of Ireland
ITALIA	a) - Tribunale di Torino	- Piemonte, Liguria, Val d'Aosta
	- Tribunale di Milano	- Lombardia, Veneto, Trentino-Alto Adige, Friuli-Venezia Giulia
	- Tribunale di Bologna	- Emilia-Romagna, Toscana, Marche
	- Tribunale di Roma	- Lazio, Umbria, Campania, Abruzzi, Molise
	- Tribunale di Bari	- Puglia, Basilicata, Calabria
	- Tribunale di Palermo	- Sicilia
	- Tribunale di Cagliari	- Sardegna

Contracting State	Name of the Court (a) First instance (b) Second instance	Territorial jurisdiction
ITALIA	b) - Corte d'appello di Torino	- Piemonte, Liguria, Val d'Aosta
	- Corte d'appello di Milano	- Lombardia, Veneto, Trentino-Alto Adige, Friuli-Venezia Giulia
	- Corte d'appello di Bologna	- Emilia-Romagna, Toscana, Marche
	- Corte d'appello di Roma	- Lazio, Umbria, Campania, Abruzzi, Molise
	- Corte d'appello di Bari	- Puglia, Basilicata, Calabria
	- Corte d'appello di Palermo	- Sicilia
	- Corte d'appello di Cagliari	- Sardegna
LUXEMBOURG	a) Tribunal d'arrondissement de Luxembourg ou de Diekirch	Tout le Luxembourg
	b) Cour d'appel du Grand-Duché	Tout le Luxembourg
NEDERLAND	a) Arrondissementsrechtbank	Hele Nederlandse grondgebied
	b) Gerechtshof te 's-Gravenhage	Hele Nederlandse grondgebied

Contracting State	Name of the Court (a) First instance (b) Second instance	Territorial jurisdiction
UNITED KINGDOM	a) - The Patent Court - The Outer House of the Court of Session - The High Court b) - The Court of Appeal - The Inner House of the Court of Session - The Court of Appeal	- England and Wales - Scotland - Northern Ireland - England and Wales - Scotland - Northern Ireland

PROTOCOL ON PRIVILEGES AND IMMUNITIES
OF THE COMMON APPEAL COURT

(Protocol on Privileges and Immunities)

Article 1

1. The premises of the Common Appeal Court, hereinafter referred to as "the Court", shall be inviolable.

2. The authorities of a State in which the Court has its premises shall not enter those premises, except with the consent of the President of the Court or his representative. Such consent shall be assumed in case of fire or other disaster requiring prompt protective action.

3. Service of process at the premises of the Court and of any other procedural instruments relating to a cause of action against the Court shall not constitute breach of inviolability.

Article 2

The archives of the Court and any documents belonging to or held by it shall be inviolable.

Article 3

1. Within the scope of its official activities the Court shall have immunity from jurisdiction except:

(a) to the extent that the Court shall have expressly waived such immunity in a particular case, given that the Court has the duty to waive such immunity where it is impeding the normal course of justice and that it is possible to dispense with such immunity without prejudicing the interests of the Court;

(b) in the case of a civil action brought by a third party for damage resulting from an accident caused by a vehicle belonging to, or operated on behalf of, the Court, or in respect of a traffic offence involving such a vehicle;

(c) in the event of the attachment, pursuant to a decision by the judicial authorities or by the administrative authorities referred to in Article Va of the Protocol annexed to the Convention of 27 September 1968 on Jurisdiction and the Enforcement of Judgments in Civil and Commercial Matters as amended by the Convention of Accession of 9 October 1978, of the salaries and emoluments, including pensions, owed by the Court to a member or former member of its staff;

(d) in the case of a civil action based on an obligation of the Court resulting from a contract, including a contract of employment concluded with a staff member;

(e) where the Court has instituted proceedings and the defendant brings a counter-action directly linked to the main action.

Article 3 (continued)

2. The official activities of the Court shall, for the purposes of this Protocol, be such as are strictly necessary for performance of the duties assigned to it by the Protocol on the Settlement of Litigation concerning the Infringement and Validity of Community Patents.

Article 4

1. The property and assets of the Court, wherever situated, shall be immune from any form of requisition, confiscation, expropriation, sequestration and execution unless the immunity of the Court is excluded by reason of a fact referred to in Article 3 paragraph 1(a) to (e).

2. The property and assets of the Court shall also be immune from any form of administrative or provisional judicial constraint, except insofar as may be temporarily necessary in connection with the prevention and investigation of accidents involving vehicles belonging to or operated on behalf of the Court and except insofar as the immunity of the Court is excluded under Article 3 paragraph 1(a) to (e).

Article 5

1. Within the scope of its official activities, the Court and its property and income shall be exempt from all direct taxes.

2. Where, for the exercise of its official activities, substantial purchases in the price of which taxes or duties are included are made by the Court, appropriate measures shall, whenever possible, be taken by the Contracting States to remit or reimburse to the Court the amount of such taxes or duties.

3. No exemption shall be accorded in respect of duties and taxes merely constituting charges for public utility services.

Article 6

Goods imported or exported by the Court for the exercise of its official activities shall be exempt from duties and charges on import or export, other than fees or taxes representing services rendered, and from all prohibitions and restrictions on import or export.

Article 7

No exemption shall be granted under Articles 5 and 6 for the personal benefit of the judges, officials or other servants of the Court.

Article 8

1. Goods belonging to the Court which have been acquired or imported under Article 5 or Article 6 shall not be sold or given away except in accordance with conditions agreed to by the Contracting States which have granted the exemptions.

2. The transfer of goods and provision of services between the various buildings of the Court shall be exempt from charges or restrictions of any kind; where appropriate, the Contracting States shall take all the necessary measures to remit or reimburse the amount of such charges or to lift such restrictions.

Article 9

The transmission of publications by or to the Court shall not be restricted in any way.

Article 10

The Court may, without being subject to any control, regulations or financial moratorium:

(a) receive and hold funds and foreign currency of any kind and have bank accounts in any of the currencies of the Member States of the European Communities or in European Currency Units,

(b) freely transfer its funds and foreign currency from one Member State of the European Communities to another or to a non-member State.

Article 11

1. For its official communications and the transmission of all its documents, the Court shall enjoy in the territory of each Contracting State the treatment accorded by that State to the Court of Justice of the European Communities.

2. Official correspondence and other official communications of the Court shall not be subject to censorship.

Article 12

The Contracting States shall take all appropriate measures to facilitate the entry, stay and departure of judges, officials and other servants of the Court.

Article 13

1. The members of the Administrative Committee, their alternates, advisers and experts shall enjoy, while attending meetings of the Administrative Committee and of any body established by it, and in the course of their journeys to and from the place of meeting, the following privileges and immunities:

(a) immunity from arrest or detention and from seizure of their personal luggage, except when found committing, attempting to commit, or just having committed an offence;

(b) immunity from jurisdiction, even after the termination of their mission, in respect of acts, including words written and spoken, done by them in the exercise of their functions; this immunity shall not apply, however, in the case of a traffic offence committed by one of the persons referred to above, or in the case of damage caused by a vehicle belonging to or driven by such a person;

(c) inviolability for all their official papers and documents;

Article 13 (continued)

(d) the right to use codes and to receive documents or correspondence by special courier or sealed bag;

(e) exemption for themselves and their spouses from all measures restricting entry and from aliens' registration formalities;

(f) the same facilities in the matter of currency and exchange control as are accorded to the representatives of foreign Governments on temporary official missions.

2. Privileges and immunities are accorded to the persons referred to in paragraph 1, not for their personal advantage but in order to ensure complete independence in the exercise of their functions in connection with the Court. Consequently, a Contracting State has the duty to waive the immunity in all cases where, in the opinion of that State, such immunity would impede the course of justice and where it can be waived without prejudicing the purposes for which it was accorded.

Article 14

The judges, officials and other servants of the Court:

(a) shall, even after their service has terminated, have immunity from jurisdiction in respect of acts, including words written and spoken, done in the exercise of their functions; this immunity shall not apply, however, in the case of a traffic offence committed by a judge, official or other servant of the Court, or in the case of damage caused by a vehicle belonging to or driven by a judge, official or other servant;

Article 14 (continued)

(b) shall be exempt from all obligations in respect of military service;

(c) shall enjoy inviolability for all their official papers and documents;

(d) shall enjoy the same facilities as regards exemption from all measures restricting immigration and governing aliens' registration as are normally accorded to staff members of international organisations, as shall members of their families forming part of their household;

(e) shall enjoy the same privileges in respect of exchange regulations as are normally accorded to the staff members of international organisations;

(f) shall enjoy the same facilities as to repatriation as diplomatic agents in times of international crisis, as shall the members of their families forming part of their household;

(g) shall have the right to import duty-free their furniture and personal effects at the time of first taking up their post in the State concerned and the right on the termination of their functions in that State to export free of duty their furniture and personal effects, subject to the conditions considered necessary by the Government of the State in whose territory the right is exercised and with the exception of property acquired in that State which is subject to an export prohibition therein.

Article 15

1. The persons referred to in Article 14 shall be subject to a tax for the benefit of the Court on salaries and emoluments paid by the Court, subject to the conditions and rules laid down by the Administrative Committee within a period of one year from the date of entry into force of the Agreement relating to Community Patents. From the date on which this tax is applied, such salaries and emoluments shall be exempt from national income tax. The Contracting States may, however, take into account the salaries and emoluments thus exempt when assessing the amount of tax to be applied to income from other sources.

2. Paragraph 1 shall not apply to pensions and annuities paid by the Court to former judges, officials or other servants of the Court.

Article 16

The Administrative Committee shall determine the categories of officials and other servants to whom the provisions of Article 14, in whole or in part, and Article 15 shall apply. The names, titles and addresses of the officials and other servants included in such categories and of the judges shall be communicated from time to time to the Contracting States.

Article 17

In the event of the Court establishing its own social security scheme, the Court, together with its judges, officials and other servants, shall be exempt from all compulsory contributions to national social security schemes, subject to the agreements made with the Contracting States in accordance with the provisions of Article 23.

Article 18

1. The privileges and immunities provided for in this Protocol are not designed to give personal advantage to judges, officials or other servants of the Court. They are provided solely to ensure, in all circumstances, the unimpeded functioning of the Court and the complete independence of the persons to whom they are accorded.

2. The Court, sitting in plenary session, has the duty to waive immunity where it considers that such immunity is impeding the normal course of justice and that it is possible to dispense with such immunity without prejudicing the interests of the Court.

Article 19

Where immunity has been waived and criminal proceedings are instituted against a judge, he shall be tried, in any of the Member States, only by the court competent to judge the members of the highest national judiciary.

Article 20

1. The Court shall cooperate at all times with the competent authorities of the Contracting States in order to facilitate the proper functioning of the processes of justice, to ensure the observance of police regulations and regulations concerning public health, labour inspection or other similar national legislation, and to prevent any abuse of the privileges, immunities and facilities provided for in this Protocol.

2. The procedure of cooperation mentioned in paragraph 1 may be laid down in the complementary agreements referred to in Article 23.

Article 21

Each Contracting State retains the right to take all precautions necessary in the interests of its security.

Article 22

No Contracting State is obliged to extend the privileges and immunities referred to in Article 13 and Article 14(b), (e) and (g) to its own nationals or permanent residents.

Article 23

The Court may, on a decision of the Administrative Committee, conclude with one or more Contracting States complementary agreements to give effect to the provisions of this Protocol as regards such State or States, and may conclude other arrangements to ensure the efficient functioning of the Court and the safeguarding of its interests.

PROTOCOL ON THE
STATUTE OF THE COMMON APPEAL COURT

Article 1

The Common Appeal Court, hereinafter referred to as "the Court", established by Article 2 of the Protocol on the Settlement of Litigation concerning the Infringement and Validity of Community Patents, hereinafter referred to as "the Protocol on Litigation", shall be constituted and shall function in accordance with the provisions of the Protocol on Litigation and of this Protocol.

PART I

JUDGES

Article 2

Before taking up his duties each judge shall, in open court, take an oath to perform his duties impartially and conscientiously and to preserve the secrecy of the deliberations of the Court.

Article 3

The judges may not hold any political or administrative office.

They may not engage in any occupation, whether gainful or not, unless exemption is exceptionally granted by the Administrative Committee.

When taking up their duties, they shall give a solemn undertaking that, both during and after their term of office, they will respect the obligations arising therefrom, in particular the duty to behave with integrity and discretion as regards the acceptance, after they have ceased to hold office, of certain appointments or benefits.

Any doubt on this point shall be settled by the Court of Justice of the European Communities.

Article 4

Apart from normal replacement, or death, the duties of a judge shall end when he resigns.

Where a judge resigns, his letter of resignation shall be addressed to the President of the Court for transmission to the Chairman of the Administrative Committee. Upon this notification a vacancy shall arise on the bench.

Save where Article 5 applies, a judge shall continue to hold office until his successor takes up his duties.

Article 5

A judge may be deprived of his office or of his right to a pension or other benefits in its stead only if, in the opinion of a three-quarters majority of the judges of the Court of Justice of the European Communities, he no longer fulfils the requisite conditions or meets the obligations arising from his office.

The initiative in respect of proceedings to that end shall lie as stipulated in the Rules of Procedure.

The President of the Court of Justice of the European Communities shall notify the decision of the Court to the Chairman of the Administrative Committee.

In the case of a decision depriving a judge of his office, a vacancy shall arise on the bench upon this notification.

Article 6

A judge who is to replace a member of the Court whose term of office has not expired shall be appointed for the remainder of his predecessor's term.

PART II

ORGANISATION

Article 7

Officials and other servants shall be attached to the Court to enable it to function. They shall be responsible to the President of the Court.

Article 8

The judges shall be required to reside at the place where the Court has its seat.

Article 9

The Court shall remain permanently in session. The duration of the judicial vacations shall be determined by the Court with due regard to the needs of its business.

Article 10

Decisions of the full Court as well as its chambers shall be valid only when an uneven number of its members is sitting in the deliberations.

Article 10 (continued)

Decisions of the full Court shall be valid if the lowest uneven number of members exceeding half of the number of members of the Court is sitting.

Decisions of the chambers shall be valid if three members are sitting; in the event of one of the judges of a chamber being prevented from attending, a judge of another chamber may be called upon to sit in accordance with the conditions laid down in the Rules of Procedure.

Article 11

No judge may take part in the disposal of any case in which he has previously taken part as adviser or has acted for one of the parties, or in which he has been called upon to pronounce as a member of a court or tribunal, of a commission of inquiry or in any other capacity.

If, for some special reason, any judge considers that he should not take part in the judgment or examination of a particular case, he shall so inform the President. If, for some special reason, the President considers that any judge should not sit in a particular case, he shall notify him accordingly.

A judge may be objected to by any party for one of the reasons mentioned in the first paragraph or if suspected of partiality.

Article 11 (continued)

A party may not apply for a change in the composition of the Court or of one of its chambers on the grounds of either the nationality of a judge or the absence from the Court or from the chamber of a judge of the nationality of that party.

Any difficulty arising as to the application of this Article shall be settled by decision of the Court.

Article 12

The parties must be represented before the Court by a lawyer entitled to practise before a court of a Contracting State.

The lawyer may be assisted by a technical adviser who is a professional representative whose name appears on the list maintained by the European Patent Office and who is entitled to act before the special departments of that Office pursuant to Article 64 of the Community Patent Convention, or by a technical adviser who is an authorised patent representative in a Contracting State. The technical adviser shall be allowed to speak at hearings under conditions laid down in the Rules of Procedure.

Such lawyers and technical advisers shall, when they appear before the Court, enjoy the rights and immunities necessary to the independent exercise of their duties, under conditions laid down in the Rules of Procedure.

As regards such lawyers and technical advisers who appear before it, the Court shall have the powers normally accorded to courts of law, under conditions laid down in the Rules of Procedure.

Article 13

The procedure before the Court shall consist of two parts: written and oral.

The written procedure shall consist of the communication to the persons involved in the proceedings of applications, statements of case, defences and observations and of replies, as well as of all papers and documents in support or of certified copies of them.

Communications shall be made by the Registry in the order and within the time laid down in the Rules of Procedure.

The oral procedure shall consist of the reading of the report presented by a judge acting as Rapporteur, the hearing by the Court of lawyers and technical advisers, as well as the hearing, if any, of witnesses and experts.

Article 14

The Court may require the parties to produce all documents and to supply all information which the Court considers desirable. Formal note shall be taken of any refusal.

Article 15

New evidence may be produced before the Court under conditions laid down in the Rules of Procedure.

Article 16

The Court may at any time entrust any individual, body, authority, committee or other organisation it chooses with the task of giving an expert opinion.

Article 17

Witnesses may be heard under conditions laid down in the Rules of Procedure.

Article 18

With respect to defaulting witnesses and experts the Court shall have the powers generally granted to courts and tribunals and may impose pecuniary penalties under conditions laid down in the Rules of Procedure.

Article 19

Witnesses and experts may be heard on oath taken in the form laid down in the Rules of Procedure or in the manner laid down by the law of the country of the witness or expert.

Article 20

The Court may order that a witness or expert be heard by the judicial authority of his place of permanent residence.

The order shall be sent for implementation to the competent judicial authority under conditions laid down in the Rules of Procedure. The documents drawn up in compliance with the letters rogatory shall be returned to the Court under the same conditions.

The Court shall defray the expenses, without prejudice to the right to charge them, where appropriate, to the parties.

Article 21

A Contracting State shall treat any violation of an oath by a witness or expert in the same manner as if the offence had been committed before one of its courts with jurisdiction in civil proceedings. At the instance of the Court, the Contracting State concerned shall prosecute the offender before its competent court.

Article 22

A hearing in court shall be public, unless the Court, of its own motion or on application by the parties, decides otherwise for serious reasons.

Article 23

During a hearing the Court may examine the experts, the witnesses and the parties themselves. The latter, however, may address the Court only through their representatives.

Article 24

Minutes shall be made of each hearing and signed by the President and a member of the Registry.

Article 25

The cause list shall be established by the President.

Article 26

The deliberations of the Court shall be and shall remain secret.

Article 27

Judgments of the Court shall state the reasons on which they are based. They shall contain the names of the judges who took part in the deliberations.

Article 28

Judgments of the Court shall be signed by the President and a member of the Registry. They shall be delivered in open court.

Article 29

Where the Court is satisfied that any person has established an interest in the result of any case submitted to the Court, the Court may allow that person to intervene in the case.

Submissions made in an application to intervene shall be limited to supporting the submissions of one of the parties.

Article 30

Periods of grace based on considerations of distance shall be determined by the Rules of Procedure.

No right shall be prejudiced in consequence of the expiry of a time limit if the party concerned proves the existence of unforeseeable circumstances or of force majeure.

Article 31

If the meaning or scope of a judgment rendered by the Court pursuant to Article 28 of the Protocol on Litigation is in doubt, the Court shall construe it on application by any party establishing an interest therein.

Article 32

The law of the Contracting State in which the Community patent court of second instance referring the case to the Court has its seat shall be applicable to the revision of a judgment rendered by the Court pursuant to Article 25 of the Protocol on Litigation. Article 23 of the Protocol on Litigation shall also be applicable to revision proceedings.

Article 64 paragraph 1 of the Community Patent Convention in conjunction with Article 125 of the European Patent Convention shall be applicable to the revision of a judgment rendered by the Court pursuant to Article 28 of the Protocol on Litigation.

Article 33

Unless otherwise provided in the Agreement relating to Community Patents or in national law, the Court and the courts or authorities of the Contracting States shall on request give assistance to each other by communicating information or opening files for inspection.

Article 34

The Rules of Procedure of the Court provided for in Article 12 of the Protocol on Litigation shall contain, apart from the provisions contemplated by this Protocol, any other provisions necessary for applying and, where required, supplementing it.

PROTOCOL
ON AMENDMENTS TO THE
COMMUNITY PATENT CONVENTION

(Protocol on Amendments)

Article 1

The Preamble to the Community Patent Convention shall be deleted.

Article 2

The following shall be substituted for Article 4:

"The following bodies common to the Contracting States shall implement the procedures laid down in this Convention:

(a) special departments which are set up within the European Patent Office and whose work shall be supervised by a Select Committee of the Administrative Council of the European Patent Organisation;

(b) the Common Appeal Court established by the Protocol on the Settlement of Litigation concerning the Infringement and Validity of Community Patents, hereinafter referred to as "the Protocol on Litigation"."

Article 3

Article 5 shall be deleted.

Article 4

Article 7 subparagraph (c) shall be deleted.

Article 5

The following shall be substituted for Article 8 paragraph 3:

"3.   The members of the Patent Administration Division may not be members of the Boards of Appeal or the Enlarged Board of Appeal set up under the European Patent Convention".

Article 6

Articles 10 to 12 shall be deleted.

Article 7

The following shall be substituted for Article 13:

"1. Members of the Revocation Divisions may not take part in any proceedings if they have any personal interest therein, if they have previously been involved as representatives of one of the parties, or if they have participated in the final decision on the case in the proceedings for grant or opposition proceedings.

2. If, for one of the reasons mentioned in paragraph 1 or for any other reason, a member of a Revocation Division considers that he should not take part in any proceedings, he shall inform the division accordingly.

3. Members of a Revocation Division may be objected to by any party for one of the reasons mentioned in paragraph 1, or if suspected of partiality. An objection shall not be admissible if, while being aware of a reason for objection, the party has taken a procedural step. No objection may be based upon the nationality of members.

4. The Revocation Divisions shall decide as to the action to be taken in the cases specified in paragraphs 2 and 3 without the participation of the member concerned. For the purposes of taking this decision the member objected to shall be replaced by his alternate."

/**Article 8**

The following shall be substituted for Article 24:/[5]

Article 9

The following shall be substituted for Article 36:

"1. The effects of a Community patent shall be governed solely by the provisions of this Convention. In other respects, infringement of a Community patent shall be governed by the national law relating to infringement of a national patent, in accordance with and subject to the provisions of the Protocol on Litigation.

2. Paragraph 1 shall apply mutatis mutandis to a European patent application which may result in the grant of a Community patent".

Article 10

The following words shall be deleted from Article 51, paragraph 4:

"or a Revocation Board".

---
[5] The content of this Article is to be decided later after examination by the Community Patent Interim Committee.

Article 11

The following shall be substituted for Article 61 paragraph 1, first sentence:

"1. Each party to revocation proceedings shall meet the costs he has incurred unless a decision of a Revocation Division in accordance with the Implementing Regulations or of the Common Appeal Court in accordance with its Rules of Procedure, for reasons of equity, orders a different apportionment of costs incurred during taking of evidence or in oral proceedings."

Article 12

The following shall be substituted for Article 62 paragraph 2:

"2. Articles 106 to 109 of the European Patent Convention shall apply *mutatis mutandis* to this appeals procedure insofar as the Rules of Procedure of the Common Appeal Court or the Rules relating to Fees do not provide otherwise."

Article 13

Article 63 shall be deleted.

Article 14

1. In Article 64 paragraph 1(a) and (b) the words "and the Revocation Boards" shall be deleted.

2. The following shall be substituted for Article 64, paragraph 1(d):

"(d) Article 123 paragraph 3 shall apply to limitation and revocation proceedings before the Revocation Divisions."

Article 15

The following shall be substituted for the title of Part VI:

"Jurisdiction and procedure in actions relating to Community patents other than those governed by the Protocol on Litigation".

Article 16

The following shall be substituted for Article 68:

"Unless otherwise specified in this Convention, the Convention on Jurisdiction and Enforcement of Judgments in Civil and Commercial Matters, signed at Brussels on 27 September 1968, as amended by the Conventions on the Accession to that Convention of the States acceding to the European Communities, the whole of which Convention and of which Conventions of Accession are hereinafter referred to as the "Convention on Jurisdiction and Enforcement", shall apply to actions relating to Community patents, other than those to which the Protocol on Litigation applies, and to decisions given in respect of such actions."

Article 17

The following shall be substituted for Article 69:

"The following courts shall have exclusive jurisdiction:

(a) in actions relating to compulsory licences in respect of a Community patent, the courts of the Contracting State the national law of which is applicable to the licence;

(b) in actions relating to the right to a patent in which an employer and an employee are in dispute, the courts of the Contracting State under whose law the right to a European patent is determined in accordance with the second sentence of Article 60 paragraph 1 of the European Patent Convention. Any agreement conferring jurisdiction shall be valid only in so far as the national law governing the contract of employment allows the agreement in question."

Article 18

Article 73 shall be deleted.

Article 19

The following shall be substituted for Article 76:

"A national court which is dealing with an action relating to a Community patent, other than the actions governed by the Protocol on Litigation, shall treat the patent as valid."

Article 20

The following shall be substituted for Article 77 paragraph 1:

"1. If the decision in an action before a national court relating to a European patent application which may result in the grant of a Community patent, other than an action governed by the Protocol on Litigation, depends upon the patentability of the invention, that decision may be given only after the European Patent Office has granted a Community patent or refused the European patent application. Paragraph 2 shall apply after the grant of the Community patent."

Article 21

Article 78 shall be deleted.

Article 22

The following shall be substituted for Article 86 paragraph 5:

"5. The decision referred to in paragraph 4 shall require unanimity."

/ Article 23

The following paragraph 2 shall be added to Article 87:

"2. When this Convention takes effect with respect to a State after its entry into force, paragraph 1 shall apply mutatis mutandis to European patent applications to which this Convention applies and in which that State is designated." /[6]

---

[6] The text in square brackets will be maintained in the event of the Agreement entering into force with fewer than twelve ratifications.

Article 24

1. In Article 88 paragraphs 1 and 6 the words "Contracting State" shall be replaced by "signatory State".

2. The following shall be substituted for Article 88 paragraph 5:

"5. Any reservation made by a signatory State under paragraph 1 shall cease to apply when the Council of the European Communities, acting unanimously on a proposal from the Commission of the European Communities or from a signatory State, decides to terminate it. / The Council may only take such a decision after the Agreement relating to Community Patents has entered into force with respect to all the signatory States./ [7] "

---
[7] The text in square brackets will be maintained in the event of the Agreement entering into force with fewer than twelve ratifications.

Article 25

1. In Article 89 paragraphs 1 and 4 the words "Contracting State" shall be replaced by "signatory State".

2. The following shall be substituted for Article 89 paragraph 2:

"2. Any reservation made by a signatory State under paragraph 1 shall have effect until the end of the tenth year at the latest after the entry into force of the Agreement relating to Community Patents /with respect to all the signatory States./[8] However, the Council of the European Communities may, acting by a qualified majority on a proposal from a signatory State, extend the period in respect of a signatory State making such a reservation by not more than five years. This majority shall be that specified in the second indent of the second subparagraph of Article 148 paragraph 2 of the Treaty establishing the European Economic Community."

---

[8] The text in square brackets will be maintained in the event of the Agreement entering into force with fewer than twelve ratifications.

Article 26

Article 90 shall be deleted.

Article 27

In Article 91 paragraph 1, the reference to Article 160 paragraph 2 of the European Patent Convention shall be deleted.

Article 28

Articles 93 to 103 inclusive shall be deleted.

Article 29

Rules 2, 3 and 30 of the Implementing Regulations shall be deleted.

Article 30

Rule 31 paragraph 2 of the Implementing Regulations shall be supplemented by the following subparagraph (h):

"(h) a record of the information communicated to the European Patent Office concerning proceedings under the Protocol on Litigation."

ANNEX

CONVENTION

FOR THE EUROPEAN PATENT

FOR THE COMMON MARKET

(Community Patent Convention)

AND IMPLEMENTING REGULATIONS

AS AMENDED BY THE PROTOCOL ON AMENDMENTS

CONVENTION

FOR THE EUROPEAN PATENT

FOR THE COMMON MARKET

(Community Patent Convention)

PART I

GENERAL AND INSTITUTIONAL PROVISIONS

CHAPTER I
General provisions

Article 1
Common system of law for patents

1. A system of law, common to the Contracting States, concerning patents for invention is hereby established.

2. The common system of law shall govern the European patents granted for the Contracting States in accordance with the Convention on the Grant of European Patents, hereinafter referred to as "the European Patent Convention", and the European patent applications in which such States are designated.

Article 2
Community patent

1. European patents granted for the Contracting States shall be called Community patents.

2. Community patents shall have a unitary character. They shall have equal effect throughout the territories to which this Convention applies and may only be granted, transferred, revoked or allowed to lapse in respect of the whole of such territories. The same shall apply mutatis mutandis to applications for European patents in which the Contracting States are designated.

Article 2 (continued)

3. Community patents shall have an autonomous character. They shall be subject only to the provisions of this Convention and those provisions of the European Patent Convention which are binding upon every European patent and which shall consequently be deemed to be provisions of this Convention.

Article 3
Joint designation

Designation of the States parties to this Convention in accordance with Article 79 of the European Patent Convention shall be effected jointly. Designation of one or some only of these States shall be deemed to be designation of all of these States.

Article 4
Setting up of special departments

The following bodies common to the Contracting States shall implement the procedures laid down in this Convention:

(a) special departments which are set up within the European Patent Office and whose work shall be supervised by a Select Committee of the Administrative Council of the European Patent Organisation;

(b) the Common Appeal Court established by the Protocol on the Settlement of Litigation concerning the Infringement and Validity of Community Patents, hereinafter referred to as "the Protocol on Litigation".

Article 5
Jurisdiction of the Court of Justice of the European Communities

– deleted –

Article 6
National patents

This Convention shall be without prejudice to the right of the Contracting States to grant national patents.

CHAPTER II

Special departments of the European Patent Office

Article 7
The special departments

The special departments shall be as follows:

(a) a Patent Administration Division;

(b) one or more Revocation Divisions.

Article 8
Patent Administration Division

1. The Patent Administration Division shall be responsible for all acts of the European Patent Office relating to Community patents, in so far as these acts are not the responsibility of other departments of the Office. It shall in particular be responsible for decisions in respect of entries in the Register of Community Patents.

2. Decisions of the Patent Administration Division shall be taken by one legally qualified member.

3. The members of the Patent Administration Division may not be members of the Boards of Appeal or the Enlarged Board of Appeal set up under the European Patent Convention.

Article 9
Revocation Divisions

1. The Revocation Divisions shall be responsible for the examination of requests for the limitation of and applications for the revocation of Community patents, and for determining compensation under Article 44 paragraph 5.

2. A Revocation Division shall consist of one legally qualified member who shall be the Chairman, and two technically qualified members. Prior to the taking of a final decision on the request or application, the Revocation Division may entrust the examination of the request or application to one of its members. Oral proceedings shall be before the Revocation Division itself.

Article 10
Revocation Boards
- deleted -

Article 11
Appointment of members of the Revocation Boards
- deleted -

Article 12
Independence of the members of the Revocation Boards
- deleted -

Article 13
Exclusion and objection

1. Members of the Revocation Divisions may not take part in any proceedings if they have any personal interest therein, if they have previously been involved as representatives of one of the parties, or if they have participated in the final decision on the case in the proceedings for grant or opposition proceedings.

2. If, for one of the reasons mentioned in paragraph 1 or for any other reason, a member of a Revocation Division considers that he should not take part in any proceedings, he shall inform the division accordingly.

3. Members of a Revocation Division may be objected to by any party for one of the reasons mentioned in paragraph 1, or if suspected of partiality. An objection shall not be admissible if, while being aware of a reason for objection, the party has taken a procedural step. No objection may be based upon the nationality of members.

Article 13 (continued)

4. The Revocation Divisions shall decide as to the action to be taken in the cases specified in paragraphs 2 and 3 without the participation of the member concerned. For the purpose of taking this decision the member objected to shall be replaced by his alternate.

Article 14
Languages for proceedings and publications

1. The official languages of the European Patent Office shall also be the official languages of the special departments.

2. Throughout the proceedings before the special departments, a translation filed in accordance with Article 14 paragraph 2 second sentence of the European Patent Convention may be brought into conformity with the original text of the European patent application.

3. The official language of the European Patent Office in which the Community patent is granted shall be used as the language of the proceedings in all proceedings before the special departments concerning the Community patent, unless otherwise provided in the Implementing Regulations.

4. However, natural or legal persons having their residence or principal place of business within the territory of a Contracting State having a language other than one of the official languages of the European Patent Office as an official language, and nationals of that State who are resident abroad, may file documents which have to be filed within a time limit in an official language of the Contracting State concerned. They must however file a translation in the language of the proceedings within the time limit prescribed in the Implementing Regulations; in the cases provided for in the Implementing Regulations, they may file a translation in a different official language of the European Patent Office.

Article 14 (continued)

5. If any document is not filed in the language prescribed by this Convention, or if any translation required by virtue of this Convention is not filed in due time, the document shall be deemed not to have been received.

6. New specifications of Community patents published following limitation or revocation proceedings shall be published in the language of the proceedings; they shall include a translation of the amended claims in one of the official languages of each of the Contracting States which do not have as an official language the language of the proceedings.

7. The Community Patent Bulletin shall be published in the three official languages of the European Patent Office.

8. Entries in the Register of Community Patents shall be made in the three official languages of the European Patent Office. In cases of doubt, the entry in the language of the proceedings shall be authentic.

9. No Contracting State may avail itself of the authorisations given in Article 65, Article 67 paragraph 3 and Article 70 paragraph 3 of the European Patent Convention.

CHAPTER III

The Select Committee of the Administrative Council

Article 15
Membership

1. The Select Committee of the Administrative Council shall be composed of the Representatives of the Contracting States, the Representative of the Commission of the European Communities and their alternate Representatives. Each Contracting State and the Commission shall be entitled to appoint one Representative and one alternate Representative to the Select Committee. The same members shall represent the Contracting States on the Administrative Council and on the Select Committee.

2. The members of the Select Committee may, subject to the provisions of its Rules of Procedure, be assisted by advisers or experts.

Article 16
Chairmanship

1. The Select Committee of the Administrative Council shall elect a Chairman and a Deputy Chairman from among the Representatives and alternate Representatives of the Contracting States. The Deputy Chairman shall <u>ex officio</u> replace the Chairman in the event of his being prevented from attending to his duties.

2. The duration of the terms of office of the Chairman and the Deputy Chairman shall be three years. The terms of office shall be renewable.

Article 17
Board

1. The Select Committee of the Administrative Council pay set up a Board composed of five of its members.

2. The Chairman and the Depty Chairman of the Select Committee shall be members of the Board ex officio; the other three members shall be elected by the Select Committee.

3. The term of office of the members elected by the Select Committee shall be three years. This term of office shall not be renewable.

4. The Board shall perform the duties given to it by the Select Committee in accordance with the Rules of Procedure.

Article 18
Meetings

1. Meetings of the Select Committee of the Administrative Council shall be convened by its Chairman.

2. The President of the European Patent Office shall take part in the deliberations of the Select Committee.

3. The Select Committee shall hold an ordinary meeting once each year. In addition, it shall meet on the initiative of its Chairman or at the request of one-third of the Contracting States.

4. The deliberations of the Select Committee shall be based on an agenda, and shall be held in accordance with its Rules of Procedure.

5. The provisional agenda shall contain any question whose inclusion is requested by any Contracting State in accordance with the Rules of Procedure.

Article 19
Languages of the Select Committee

1. The languages in use in the deliberations of the Select Committee of the Administrative Council shall be English, French and German.

2. Documents submitted to the Select Committee, and the minutes of its deliberations, shall be drawn up in the three languages mentioned in paragraph 1.

Article 20
Competence of the Select Committee in certain cases

1. The Select Committee of the Administrative Council shall be competent to amend the following provisions of this Convention:

   (a) the time limits laid down in the Convention which are to be observed vis-à-vis the European Patent Office;

   (b) the Implementing Regulations.

2. The Select Committee shall be competent, in conformity with this Convention, to adopt or amend the following provisions:

   (a) the Financial Regulations;

   (b) the Rules relating to Fees;

   (c) its Rules of Procedure.

Article 21
Voting rights

1. The right to vote in the Select Committee of the Administrative Council shall be restricted to the Contracting States.

2. Each Contracting State shall have one vote, subject to the application of the provisions of Article 23.

Article 22
Voting Rules

1. The Select Committee of the Administrative Council shall take its decisions other than those referred to in paragraph 2 by a simple majority of the Contracting States represented and voting.

2. A majority of three-quarters of the votes of the Contracting States represented and voting shall be required for the decisions which the Select Committee is empowered to take under Article 20 and Article 25 subparagraph (a).

3. Abstentions shall not be considered as votes.

Article 23
Weighting of votes

In respect of the adoption or amendment of the Rules relating to Fees and, if the financial contribution to be made by the Contracting States would thereby be increased, the approval referred to in Article 25 subparagraph (a), voting shall be conducted according to Article 36 of the European Patent Convention. The term "Contracting States" in that Article shall be understood as meaning the States parties to this Convention.

CHAPTER IV

Financial provisions

Article 24
Financial obligations and benefits[9]

Article 25
Powers of the Select Committee of the
Administrative Council in budgetary matters

The Select Committee of the Administrative Council shall:

(a) approve annually the forecasts of expenditure and revenue relating to the implementation of this Convention and any amendments or additions made to these forecasts, submitted to it by the President of the European Patent Office, and supervise the implementation thereof;

(b) grant the authorisation provided for in Article 47 paragraph 2 of the European Patent Convention, insofar as the expenditure involved relates to the implementation of this Convention;

(c) approve the annual accounts of the European Patent Organisation which relate to the implementation of this Convention and that part of the report of the auditors appointed under Article 49 paragraph 1 of the European Patent Convention which relates to these accounts, and give the President of the European Patent Office a discharge.

---

[9] The content of this Article is to be decided later after examination by the Community Patent Interim Committee.

Article 26
Rules relating to fees

The Rules relating to Fees shall determine in particular the amounts of the fees and the ways in which they are to be paid.

PART II

SUBSTANTIVE PATENT LAW

CHAPTER I
Right to the Community patent

Article 27
Claiming the right to the Community patent

1. If a Community patent has been granted to a person who is not entitled to it under Article 60 paragraph 1 of the European Patent Convention, the person entitled to it under that provision may, without prejudice to any other remedy which may be open to him, claim to have the patent transferred to him.

2. Where a person is entitled to only part of the Community patent, that person may, in accordance with paragraph 1, claim to be made a joint proprietor.

3. Legal proceedings in respect of the rights specified in paragraphs 1 and 2 may be instituted only within a period of not more than two years after the date on which the European Patent Bulletin mentions the grant of the European patent. This provision shall not apply if the proprietor of the patent knew, at the time when the patent was granted or transferred to him, that he was not entitled to the patent.

Article 27 (continued)

4. The fact that legal proceedings have been instituted shall be entered in the Register of Community Patents. Entry shall also be made of the final decision in, or of any other termination of, the proceedings.

Article 28
Effect of change of proprietorship

1. Where there is a complete change of proprietorship of a Community patent as a result of legal proceedings under Article 27, licences and other rights shall lapse upon the registration of the person entitled to the patent in the Register of Community Patents.

2. If, before the institution of legal proceedings has been registered,

   (a) the proprietor of the patent has used the invention within the territory of any of the Contracting States or made effective and serious preparations to do so, or

   (b) a licensee of the patent has obtained his licence and has used the invention within the territory of any of the Contracting States or made effective and serious preparations to do so,

   he may continue such use provided that he requests a non-exclusive licence of the patent from the new proprietor whose name is entered in the Register of Community Patents. Such request must be made within the period prescribed in the Implementing Regulations. The licence shall be granted for a reasonable period and upon reasonable terms.

Article 28 (continued)

3. Paragraph 2 shall not apply if the proprietor of the patent or the licensee, as the case may be, was acting in bad faith at the time when he began to use the invention or to make preparations to do so.

CHAPTER II

Effects of the Community patent
and the European patent application

Article 29
Prohibition of direct use of the invention

A Community patent shall confer on its proprietor the right to prevent all third parties not having his consent:

(a) from making, offering, putting on the market or using a product which is the subject-matter of the patent, or importing or stocking the product for these purposes;

(b) from using a process which is the subject-matter of the patent or, when the third party knows, or it is obvious in the circumstances, that the use of the process is prohibited whithout the consent of the proprietor of the patent, from offering the process for use within the territories of the Contracting States;

(c) from offering, putting on the market, using, or importing or stocking for these purposes the product obtained directly by a process which is the subject-matter of the patent.

Article 30
Prohibition of indirect use of the invention

1. A Community patent shall also confer on its proprietor the right to prevent all third parties not having his consent from supplying or offering to supply within the territories of the Contracting States a person, other than a party entitled to exploit the patented invention, with means, relating to an essential element of that invention, for putting it into effect therein, when the third party knows, or it is obvious in the circumstances, that these means are suitable and intended for putting that invention into effect.

2. Paragraph 1 shall not apply when the means are staple commercial products, except when the third party induces the person supplied to commit acts prohibited by Article 29.

3. Persons performing the acts referred to in Article 31 subparagraphs (a) to (c) shall not be considered to be parties entitled to exploit the invention within the meaning of paragraph 1.

Article 31
Limitation of the effects of the Community patent

The rights conferred by a Community patent shall not extend to:

(a) acts done privately and for non-commercial purposes;

(b) acts done for experimental purposes relating to the subject-matter of the patented invention;

(c) the extemporaneous preparation for individual cases in a pharmacy of a medicine in accordance with a medical prescription nor acts concerning the medicine so prepared;

Article 31 (continued)

(d) the use on board vessels of the countries of the Union of Paris for the Protection of Industrial Property, other than the Contracting States, of the patented invention, in the body of the vessel, in the machinery, tackle, gear and other accessories, when such vessels temporarily or accidentally enter the waters of Contracting States, provided that the invention is used there exclusively for the needs of the vessel;

(e) the use of the patented invention in the construction or operation of aircraft or land vehicles of countries of the Union of Paris for the Protection of Industrial Property, other than the Contracting States, or of accessories to such aircraft or land vehicles, when these temporarily or accidentally enter the territory of Contracting States;

(f) the acts specified in Article 27 of the Convention on International Civil Aviation of 7 December 1944, where these acts concern the aircraft of a State, other than the Contracting States, benefiting from the provisions of that Article.

Article 32
Exhaustion of the rights conferred by the Community patent

The rights conferred by a Community patent shall not extend to acts concerning a product covered by that patent which are done within the territories of the Contracting States after that product has been put on the market in one of these States by the proprietor of the patent or with his express consent, unless there are grounds which, under Community law, would justify the extension to such acts of the rights conferred by the patent.

Article 33
Translation of the claims in
examination or opposition proceedings

1. The applicant shall file with the European Patent Office within the time limit prescribed in the Implementing Regulations a translation of the claims on which the grant of the European patent is to be based in one of the official languages of each of the Contracting States which does not have English, French or German as an official language.

2. Paragraph 1 shall apply mutatis mutandis in respect of claims which are amended during opposition proceedings.

3. The translations of the claims shall be published by the European Patent Office.

4. The applicant for or proprietor of the patent shall pay the fee for the publication of the translations of the claims within the time limits prescribed in the Implementing Regulations.

5. If the translations prescribed in paragraphs 1 and 2 are not filed in due time or if the fee for the publication of the translations of the claims is not paid in due time, the Community patent shall be deemed to be void ab initio, unless these acts are done and the additional fee is paid within a further period as prescribed in the Implementing Regulations.

Article 34
Rights conferred by a European patent application after publication

1. Compensation reasonable in the circumstances may be claimed from a third party who, in the period between the date of publication of a European patent application in which the Contracting States are designated and the date of publication of the mention of the grant of the European patent, has made any use of the invention which, after that period, would be prohibited by virtue of the Community patent.

2. Any Contracting State which does not have as an official language the language of the proceedings of a European patent application in which the Contracting States are designated, may prescribe that such application shall not confer, in respect of use of the invention within its territory, the right referred to in paragraph 1 until such time as the applicant, at his option, has:

   (a) supplied a translation of the claims in one if its official languages to the competent authority of that State and the translation has been published, or

   (b) communicated such a translation to the person using the invention within that State.

Article 35
Effect of revocation of the Community patent

1. A European patent application in which the Contracting States are designated and the resulting Community patent shall be deemed not to have had, as from the outset, the effects specified in this Chapter, to the extent that the patent has been revoked.

Article 35 (continued)

2. Subject to the national provisions relating either to claims for compensation for damage caused by negligence or lack of good faith on the part of the proprietor of the patent, or to unjust enrichment, the retroactive effect of the revocation of the patent as a result of opposition or revocation proceedings shall not affect:

(a) any decision on infringement which has acquired the authority of a final decision and been enforced prior to the revocation decision;

(b) any contract concluded prior to the revocation decision, in so far as it has been performed before that decision; however, repayment, to an extent justified by the circumstances, of sums paid under the relevant contract, may be claimed on grounds of equity.

Article 36
Complementary application of national law regarding infringement

1. The effects of a Community patent shall be governed solely by the provisions of this Convention. In other respects, infringement of a Community patent shall be governed by the national law relating to infringement of a national patent, in accordance with and subject to the provisions of the Protocol on Litigation.

2. Paragraph 1 shall apply *mutatis mutandis* to a European patent application which may result in the grant of a Community patent.

CHAPTER III

National rights

Article 37
National prior right

1. With regard to a Community patent having a date of filing or, where priority has been claimed, a date of priority later than that of a national patent application or national patent made public in a Contracting State on or after that date, the national patent application or patent shall, for that Contracting State, have the same prior right effect as a published European patent application designating that Contracting State.

2. If, in a Contracting State, a national patent application or patent, which is unpublished by reason of the national law of that State concerning the secrecy of inventions, has a prior right effect with regard to a national patent in that State having a later date of filing, or where priority has been claimed a later date of priority, the same shall apply in that State with regard to a Community patent.

Article 38
Right base on prior use and right of personal possession

1. Any person who, if a national patent had been granted in respect of an invention, would have had, in one of the Contracting States, a right based on prior use of that invention or a right of personal possession of that invention, shall enjoy, in that State, the same rights in respect of a Community patent for the same invention.

Article 38 (continued)

2. The rights conferred by a Community patent shall not extend to acts concerning a product covered by that patent which are done within the territory of the State concerned after that product has been put on the market in that State by the person referred to in paragraph 1, in so far as the national law of that State makes provision to the same effect in respect of national patents.

CHAPTER IV

The Community patent as an object of property

Article 39
Dealing with the Community patent as a national patent

1. Unless otherwise specified in this Convention, a Community patent as an object of property shall be dealt with in its entirety, and for the whole of the territories in which it is effective, as a national patent of the Contracting State in which, according to the Register of European Patents provided for in the European Patent Convention:

   (a) the applicant for the patent had his residence or principal place of business on the date of filing of the European patent application,

   (b) where subparagrah (a) does not apply, the applicant had a place of business on that date, or

   (c) where neither subparagraph (a) nor subparagraph (b) applies, the applicant's representative whose name is entered first in the Register of European Patents had his place of business on the date of that entry.

2. Where subparagraphs (a), (b) and (c) of paragraph 1 do not apply, the Contracting State referred to in that paragraph shall be the Federal Republic of Germany.

Article 39 (continued)

3. If two or more persons are mentioned in the Register of European Patents as joint applicants, paragraph 1 shall apply to the joint applicant first mentioned; if this is not possible, it shall apply to the joint applicant next mentioned in respect of whom it is applicable. Where paragraph 1 does not apply to any of the joint applicants, paragraph 2 shall apply.

4. If in a Contracting State as determined by the preceding paragraphs a right in respect of a national patent is effective only after entry in the national patent register, such a right in respect of a Community patent shall be effective only after entry in the Register of Community Patents.

Article 40
Transfer

1. An assignment of a Community patent shall be made in writing and shall require the signature of the parties to the contract, except when it is a result of a judgment.

2. Subject to Article 28 paragraph 1 a transfer shall not affect rights acquired by third parties before the date of transfer.

3. A transfer shall, to the extent to which it is verified by the papers referred to in the Implementing Regulations, only have effect vis-à-vis third parties after entry in the Register of Community Patents. Nevertheless, a transfer, before it is so entered, shall have effect vis-à-vis third parties who have acquired rights after the date of the transfer but who knew of the transfer at the date on which the rights were acquired.

Article 41
Enforcement proceedings

The courts and other authorities of the Contracting State determined in accordance with Article 39 shall have exclusive jurisdiction in respect of proceedings relating to judgments or other official acts in so far as they are being enforced against Community patents.

Article 42
Bankruptcy or like proceedings

1. Until such time as common rules for the Contracting States in this field enter into force, the only Contracting State in which a Community patent may be involved in bankruptcy or like proceedings shall be that in which such proceedings are opened first.

2. Paragraph 1 shall apply mutatis mutandis in the case of joint proprietorship of a Community patent to the share of the joint proprietor.

Article 43
Contractual licensing

1. A Community patent may be licensed in whole or in part for the whole or part of the territories in which it is effective. A licence may be exclusive or non-exclusive.

2. The rights conferred by the Community patent may be invoked against a licensee who contravenes any restriction in his licence which is covered by paragraph 1.

3. Article 40 paragraphs 2 and 3 shall apply mutatis mutandis to the grant or transfer of a licence in respect of a Community patent.

Article 44
Licences of right

1. Where the proprietor of a Community patent files a written statement with the European Patent Office that he is prepared to allow any person to use the invention as a licensee in return for appropriate compensation, the renewal fees for the Community patent which fall due after receipt of the statement shall be reduced; the amount of the reduction shall be fixed in the Rules relating to Fees. Where there is a complete change of proprietorship of the patent as a result of legal proceedings under Article 27, the statement shall be deemed withdrawn upon the entry of the name of the person entitled to the patent in the Register of Community Patents.

2. The statement may be withdrawn at any time upon written notification to this effect to the European Patent Office, provided that no one has informed the proprietor of the patent of his intention to use the invention. Such withdrawal shall take effect from the date of its notification. The amount by which the renewal fees were reduced shall be paid within one month after withdrawal; Article 49 paragraph 2 shall apply, but the six-month period shall start upon expiry of the above period.

3. The statement may not be filed while an exclusive licence is recorded in the Register of Community Patents or a request for the recording of such a licence is before the European Patent Office.

4. On the basis of the statement, any person shall be entitled to use the invention as a licensee under the conditions laid down in the Implementing Regulations. A licence so obtained shall, for the purposes of this Convention, be treated as a contractual licence.

Article 44 (continued)

5. On written request by one of the parties, a Revocation Division shall determine the appropriate compensation or review it if circumstances have arisen or become known which render the compensation determined obviously inappropriate. The provisions governing revocation proceedings shall apply mutatis mutandis, unless they are inapplicable as a result of the particular nature of revocation proceedings. The request shall not be deemed to have been made until such time as an administrative fee has been paid.

6. No request for recording an exclusive licence in the Register of Community Patents shall be admissible after the statement has been filed, unless it is withdrawn or deemed withdrawn.

Article 45
The European patent application as an object of property

1. Articles 39 to 43 shall apply mutatis mutandis to a European patent application in which the Contracting States are designated, the reference to the Register of Community Patents being understood as referring to the Register of European Patents provided for in the European Patent Convention.

2. The rights acquired by third parties in respect of a European patent application referred to in paragraph 1 shall continue to be effective with regard to the Community patent granted upon that application.

CHAPTER V

Compulsory licences in respect of a Community patent

Article 46
Compulsory licences

1. Any provision in the law of a Contracting State for the grant of compulsory licences in respect of national patents shall be applicable to Community patents. The extent and effect of compulsory licences granted in respect of Community patents shall be restricted to the territory of the State concerned. Article 32 shall not apply.

2. Each Contracting State shall, at least in respect of compensation under a compulsory licence, provide for a final appeal to a court of law.

3. As far as practicable national authorities shall notify the European Patent Office of the grant of any compulsory licence in respect of a Community patent.

4. For the purposes of this Convention, the term "compulsory licences" shall be construed as including official licences and any right to use patented inventions in the public interest.

Article 47
Compulsory licences for lack or insufficiency of exploitation

A compulsory licence may not be granted in respect of a Community patent on the ground of lack or insufficiency of exploitation if the product covered by the patent, which is manufactured in a Contracting State, is put on the market in the territory of any other Contracting State, for which such a licence has been requested, in sufficient quantity to satisfy needs in the territory of that other Contracting State. This provision shall not apply to compulsory licences granted in the public interest.

Article 48
Compulsory licences in respect of dependent patents

Any provisions in the law of a Contracting State for the grant of compulsory licences in respect of earlier patents in favour of subsequent dependent patents shall be applicable to the relationship between Community patents and national patents and to the relationship between Community patents themselves.

PART III

RENEWAL, LAPSE, LIMITATION AND REVOCATION OF THE COMMUNITY PATENT

CHAPTER I

Renewal and lapse

Article 49
Renewal fees

1. Renewal fees in respect of Community patents shall be paid to the European Patent Office in accordance with the Implementing Regulations. These fees shall be due in respect of the years following the year referred to in Article 86 paragraph 4 of the European Patent Convention, provided that no renewal fees shall be due in respect of the first two years, calculated from the date of filing of the application.

2. When a renewal fee has not been paid on or before the due date, the fee may be validly paid within six months of that date, provided that the additional fee is paid at the same time.

3. Any renewal fee in respect of a Community patent falling due within two months after the publication of the mention of the grant of the European patent shall be deemed to have been validly paid if it is paid within that period. No additional fee shall be charged.

Article 50

Surrender

1. A Community patent may be surrendered only in its entirety.

2. The surrender must be declared in writing to the European Patent Office by the proprietor of the patent. It shall not have effect until it is entered in the Register of Community Patents.

3. Surrender will be entered in the Register of Community Patents only with the agreement of any third party who has a right in rem recorded in the Register or in respect of whom there is an entry in the Register pursuant to Article 27 paragraph 4 first sentence. If a licence is recorded in the Register, surrender will be entered only if the proprietor of the patent proves that he has previously informed the licensee of his intention to surrender; this entry will be made on expiry of the priod laid down in the Implementing Regulations.

Article 51

Lapse

1. A Community patent shall lapse:

(a) at the end of the term laid down in Article 63 of the European Patent Convention;

(b) if the proprietor of the patent surrenders it in accordance with Article 50;

(c) if a renewal fee and any additional fee have not been paid in due time.

Article 51 (contd.)

2. The Community patent shall lapse on the date mentioned in Article 54 paragraph 4 to the extent that it is not maintained.

3. The lapse of a patent for failure to pay a renewal fee and any additional fee within the due period shall be deemed to have occurred on the date on which the renewal fee was due.

4. The lapse of a Community patent shall, if necessary, be decided by the Patent Administration Division or, if proceedings in respect of that patent are pending before it, a Revocation Division.

CHAPTER II

Limitation procedure

Article 52
Request for limitation

1. At the request of the proprietor, a Community patent may be limited in the form of an amendment to the claims, the description or the drawings. Limitation in respect of one or some of the Contracting States may be requested only where Article 37 paragraph 1 applies.

2. The request may not be filed during the period within which an opposition may be filed or while opposition proceedings or revocation proceedings are pending.

Article 52 (contd.)

3. The request shall be filed in writing with the European Patent Office. It shall not be deemed to have been filed until the fee for limitation has been paid.

4. Article 50, paragraph 3, shall apply *mutatis mutandis* to the filing of the request.

5. Where an application for revocation of the Community patent is filed during limitation proceedings, the Revocation Division shall stay the limitation proceedings until a final decision is given in respect of the application for revocation.

Article 53
Examination of the request

1. The Revocation Division shall examine whether the grounds for revocation mentioned in Article 57 paragraph 1(a) to (d) would prejudice the maintenance of the Community patent as amended.

2. In the examination of the request, which shall be conducted in accordance with the Implementing Regulations, the Revocation Division shall invite the proprietor of the patent, as often as necessary, to file observations, within a period to be fixed by the Revocation Division, on communications issued by itself.

3. If the proprietor of the patent fails to reply in due time to any invitation under paragraph 2, the request shall be deemed to be withdrawn.

Article 54
Rejection of the request or limitation
of the Community patent

1. If, following the examination provided for in Article 53, the Revocation Division is of the opinion that the amendments are not acceptable, it shall reject the request.

2. If the Revocation Division is of the opinion that, taking into consideration the amendments made by the proprietor of the patent during the limitation proceedings, the grounds for revocation mentioned in Article 57 do not prejudice the maintenance of the Community patent, it shall decide to limit the patent accordingly, provided that:

    (a) it is established, in accordance with the Implementing Regulations, that the proprietor of the patent approves the text in which the Revocation Division intends to limit the patent;

    (b) a translation of any amended claims in one of the official languages of each of the Contracting States which do not have as an official language the language of the proceedings is filed within the time limit prescribed in the Implementing Regulations;

    (c) the fee for the printing of a new specification is paid within the time limit prescribed in the Implementing Regulations.

3. If a translation is not filed in due time or if the fee for the printing of a new specification is not paid in due time, the request shall be deemed to be withdrawn, unless these acts are done and the additional fee is paid within a further period as prescribed in the Implementing Regulations.

4. The decision to limit a Community patent shall not take effect until the date on which the Community Patent Bulletin mentions the limitation.

Article 55
Publication of a new specification
following limitation proceedings

If a Community patent is limited under Article 54, paragraph 2, the European Patent Office shall, at the same time as it publishes the mention of the decision to limit, publish a new specification of the Community patent containing the description, the claims and any drawings, in the amended form.

CHAPTER III

Revocation procedure

Article 56
Application for revocation

1. Any person may file with the European Patent Office an application for revocation of a Community patent; however, in the case specified in Article 57 paragraph 1(e) the application may be filed only by a person entitled to be entered in the Register of Community Patents as the sole proprietor of the patent or by all the persons entitled to be entered as joint proprietors of it in accordance with Article 27 acting jointly.

2. The application may not be filed in the cases specified in Article 57 paragraph 1(a) to (d) during the period within which an opposition may be filed or while opposition proceedings are pending.

3. An application may be filed even if the Community patent has lapsed.

Article 56 (contd.)

4. The application shall be filed in a written reasoned statement. It shall not be deemed to have been filed until the revocation fee has been paid.

5. Applicants shall be parties to the revocation proceedings as well as the proprietor of the patent.

6. If the applicant has neither his residence nor his principal place of business within the territory of one of the Contracting States, he shall, at the request of the proprietor of the patent, furnish security for the costs of the proceedings. The Revocation Division shall fix at a reasonable figure the amount of the security and the period within which it must be deposited. If the security is not deposited within the period specified, the application shall be deemed to be withdrawn.

Article 57
Grounds for revocation

1. An application for revocation of a Community patent may be filed only on the grounds that:

    (a) the subject-matter of the patent is not patentable within the terms of Articles 52 to 57 of the European Patent Convention;

    (b) the patent does not disclose the invention in a manner sufficiently clear and complete for it to be carried out by a person skilled in the art;

    (c) the subject-matter of the patent extends beyond the content of the European patent application as filed, or, if the patent was granted on a European divisional application or on a new European application filed in accordance with Article 61 of the European Patent Convention, beyond the content of the earlier application as filed;

Article 57 (contd.)

    (d) the protection conferred by the patent has been extended;

    (e) the proprietor of the patent is not, having regard to a decision which has to be recognised in all the Contracting States, entitled under Article 60 paragraph 1 of the European Patent Convention;

    (f) the subject-matter of the patent is not patentable within the terms of Article 37 paragraph 1.

2. If the grounds for revocation affect the patent only partially, revocation shall be pronounced in the form of a corresponding limitation of the patent. The limitation may be effected in the form of an amendment to the claims, the description or the drawings.

3. In the case specified in paragraph 1(f), revocation shall be pronounced only in respect of the Contracting State in which the national patent application or national patent has been made public.

Article 58
Examination of the application

1. If the application for revocation of the Community patent is admissible, the Revocation Division shall examine whether the grounds for revocation mentioned in Article 57 prejudice the maintenance of the patent.

2. In the examination of the application, which shall be conducted in accordance with the Implementing Regulations, the Revocation Division shall invite the parties, as often as necessary, to file observations, within a period to be fixed by the Revocation Division, on communications from another party or issued by itself.

Article 59
Revocation or maintenance of the Community patent

1. If the Revocation Division is of the opinion that the grounds for revocation mentioned in Article 57 prejudice the maintenance of the Community patent, it shall revoke the patent.

2. If the Revocation Division is of the opinion that the grounds for revocation mentioned in Article 57 do not prejudice the maintenance of the patent unamended, it shall reject the application.

3. If the Revocation Division is of the opinion that, taking into consideration the amendments made by the proprietor of the patent during the revocation proceedings, the grounds for revocation mentioned in Article 57 do not prejudice the maintenance of the patent, it shall decide to maintain the patent as amended, provided that:

    (a) it is established, in accordance with the Implementing Regulations, that the proprietor of the patent approves the text in which the Revocation Division intends to maintain the patent;

    (b) a translation of any amended claims in one of the official languages of each of the Contracting States which do not have as an official language the language of the proceedings is filed within the time limit prescribed in the Implementing Regulations;

    (c) the fee for the printing of a new specification is paid within the time limit prescribed in the Implementing Regulations.

4. If a translation is not filed in due time or if the fee for the printing of a new specification is not paid in due time, the patent shall be revoked, unless these acts are done and the additional fee is paid within a further period as prescribed in the Implementing Regulations.

Article 60
Publication of a new specification
following revocation proceedings

If a Community patent is amended under Article 59 paragraph 3 the European Patent Office shall, at the same time as it publishes the mention of the decision on the application for revocation, publish a new specification of the Community patent containing the description, the claims and any drawings, in the amended form.

Article 61
Costs

1. Each party to revocation proceedings shall meet the costs he has incurred unless a decision of a Revocation Division in accordance with the Implementing Regulations or of the Common Appeal Court in accordance with its Rules of Procedure, for reasons of equity, orders a different apportionment of costs incurred during taking of evidence or in oral proceedings. A decision on the apportionment of the costs may also be taken on request when the application for revocation is withdrawn or when the Community patent lapses.

2. On request, the registry of the Revocation Division shall fix the amount of the costs to be paid under a decision apportioning them. The fixing of the costs by the registry may be reviewed by a decision of the Revocation Division on a request filed within the period laid down in the Implementing Regulations.

3. Article 104 paragraph 3 of the European Patent Convention shall apply mutatis mutandis.

PART IV

APPEALS PROCEDURE

Article 62
Appeal

1. An appeal shall lie from decisions of the Revocation Division and the Patent Administration Division.

2. Articles 106 to 109 of the European Patent Convention shall apply *mutatis mutandis* to this appeals procedure insofar as the Rules of Procedure of the Common Appeal Court or the Rules relating to Fees do not provide otherwise.

Article 63
Further appeal

– deleted –

PART V

COMMON PROVISIONS

Article 64
Common provisions governing procedure and representation

1. The provisions of Part VII, Chapters I and III, of the European Patent Convention, other than Articles 121 and 124, shall apply *mutatis mutandis* to this Convention, subject to the following:

Article 64 (contd.)

(a) Article 114 paragraph 1 shall apply only to the Revocation Divisions;

(b) Article 116 paragraphs 2 and 3 shall apply only to the Patent Administration Division, and paragraph 4 shall apply only to the Revocation Divisions;

(c) Article 122 shall also apply to all other parties to proceedings before the special departments;

(d) Article 123 paragraph 3 shall apply to limitation and revocation proceedings before the Revocation Divisions;

(e) the term "Contracting States" shall be understood as meaning the States parties to this Convention.

2. Notwithstanding paragraph 1(e), a person whose name appears on the list of professional representatives maintained by the European Patent Office who is not a national of one of the States parties to this Convention or does not have his place of business or employment within the territory of one of these States, shall be entitled to act as a professional representative for a party to proceedings relating to a Community patent before the special departments, provided that:

(a) he was, according to the Register of European Patents, the person last authorised to act as the professional representative for the same party or his predecessor in title in proceedings pursuant to the European Patent Convention which relate to this Community patent or to the European patent application on which it is based; and

Article 64 (cont.)

(b) the State of which he is a national or within the territory of which he has his place of business or employment applies rules, as regards representation before the central industrial property office of the State concerned, which comply, in respect of reciprocity, with such conditions as the Select Committee of the Administrative Council may prescribe.

Article 65
Register of Community Patents

The European Patent Office shall keep a register, to be known as the Register of Community Patents, which shall contain those particulars the registration of which is provided for by this Convention. The Register shall be open to public inspection.

Article 66
Community Patent Bulletin

The European Patent Office shall periodically publish a Community Patent Bulletin containing entries made in the Register of Community Patents, as well as other particulars, the publication of which is prescribed by this Convention.

Article 67
Information to the public or official authorities

Article 128 paragraph 4 and Articles 130 to 132 of the European Patent Convention shall apply mutatis mutandis, the term "Contracting States" being understood as meaning the States parties to this Convention.

PART VI

JURISDICTION AND PROCEDURE IN ACTIONS RELATING TO COMMUNITY PATENTS OTHER THAN THOSE GOVERNED BY THE PROTOCOL ON LITIGATION

CHAPTER I

Jurisdiction and enforcement

Article 68
General provisions

Unless otherwise specified in this Convention, the Convention on Jurisdiction and Enforcement of Judgments in Civil and Commercial Matters, signed at Brussels on 27 September 1968, as amended by the Conventions on the Accession to that Convention of the States acceding to the European Communities, the whole of which Convention and of which Conventions of Accession are hereinafter referred to as the "Convention on Jurisdiction and Enforcement", shall apply to actions relating to Community patents, other than those to which the Protocol on Litigation applies, and to decisions given in respect of such actions.

Article 69
Jurisdiction of national courts concerning actions relating to Community patents

The following courts shall have exclusive jurisdiction:

(a) in actions relating to compulsory licences in respect of a Community patent, the courts of the Contracting State the national law of which is applicable to the licence;

(b) in actions relating to the right to a patent in which an employer and an employee are in dispute, the courts of the Contracting State under whose law the right to a European patent is determined in accordance with the second sentence of Article 60 paragraph 1 of the European Patent Convention. Any agreement conferring jurisdiction shall be valid only in so far as the national law governing the contract of employment allows the agreement in question.

Article 70
Supplementary provisions on jurisdiction

1. Within the Contracting State whose courts have jurisdiction under Articles 68 and 69, those courts shall have jurisdiction which would have jurisdiction *ratione loci* and *ratione materiae* in the case of actions relating to a national patent granted in that State.

2. Articles 68 and 69 shall apply to actions relating to a European patent application in which the Contracting States are designated, except in so far as the right to the grant of a European patent is claimed.

Article 70 (contd.)

3. Actions relating to a Community patent for which no court has jurisdiction under Articles 68 and 69 and paragraphs 1 and 2 may be heard before the courts of the Federal Republic of Germany.

Article 71
Supplementary provisions on recognition and enforcement

1. Article 27 paragraphs 3 and 4 of the Convention on Jurisdiction and Enforcement shall not apply to decisions relating to the right to the Community patent.

2. In the case of irreconcilable decisions relating to the right to a Community patent given in proceedings between the same parties, only the decision of the court first seised of the matter shall be recognised. Neither party may invoke any other decision even in the Contracting State in which it was given.

Article 72
National authorities

For actions relating to the right to a Community patent or to compulsory licences in respect of a Community patent the term "courts" in this Convention and the Convention on Jurisdiction and Enforcement shall include authorities which, under the national law of a Contracting State, have jurisdiction to decide such actions relating to a national patent granted in that State. Any Contracting State shall notify the European Patent Office of any authority on which such jurisdiction is conferred and the European Patent Office shall inform the other Contracting States accordingly.

Article 73
Preliminary ruling by the Court of Justice of the European Communities

- deleted -

CHAPTER II
Procedure

Article 74
Rules of procedure

Unless otherwise specified in this Convention, the actions referred to in Articles 68 to 70 shall be subject to the national rules of procedure governing the same type of action relating to a national patent.

Article 75
Burden of proof

1. If the subject-matter of a Community patent is a process for obtaining a new product, the same product when produced by any other party shall, in the absence of proof to the contrary, be deemed to have been obtained by the patented process.

2. In the adduction of proof to the contrary, the legitimate interests of the defendant in protecting his manufacturing and business secrets shall be taken into account.

Article 76
Obligation of the national court

A national court which is dealing with an action relating to a Community patent, other than the actions governed by the Protocol on Litigation, shall treat the patent as valid.

Article 77
Stay of proceedings

1. If the decision in an action before a national court relating to a European patent application which may result in the grant of a Community patent, other than an action governed by the Protocol on Litigation, depends upon the patentability of the invention, that decision may be given only after the European Patent Office has granted a Community patent or refused the European patent application. Paragraph 2 shall apply after the grant of the Community patent.

2. Where an opposition has been filed, or a request for the limitation or an application for the revocation of a Community patent has been made, the national court may, at the request of one of the parties and after hearing the other parties, stay proceedings relating to the Community patent, in so far as its decision depends upon validity. At the request of one of the parties the court shall instruct that the documentary evidence of the opposition, limitation or revocation proceedings be communicated to it, in order to give a ruling on the request for a stay of proceedings.

Article 78
Opinion on the extent of protection

– deleted –

Article 79
Penal sanctions for infringement

The national penal provisions in the matter of infringement shall be applicable in the case of infringement of a Community patent, to the extent that like acts of infringement would be punishable if they similarly affected a national patent.

PART VII

IMPACT ON NATIONAL LAW

Article 80
Prohibition of simultaneous protection

1. Where a national patent granted in a Contracting State relates to an invention for which a Community patent has been granted to the same inventor or to his successor in title with the same date of filing, or, if priority has been claimed, with the same date of priority, that national patent shall be ineffective to the extent that it covers the same invention as the Community patent, from the date on which:

    (a) the period for filing an opposition to the Community patent has expired without any opposition being filed,

    (b) the opposition proceedings are concluded with a decision to maintain the Community patent, or

    (c) the national patent is granted, where this date is subsequent to the date referred to in subparagraph (a) or (b), as the case may be.

2. The subsequent lapse or revocation of the Community patent shall not affect the provisions of paragraph 1.

Article 80 (continued

3. Each Contracting State may prescribe the procedure whereby the loss of effect of the national patent is determined and, where appropriate, the extent of that loss. It may also prescribe that the loss of effect shall apply as from the outset.

4. Prior to the date applicable under paragraph 1, simultaneous protection by a Community patent or a European patent application and a national patent or a national patent application shall exist unless any Contracting State provides otherwise.

Article 81
Exhaustion of the rights
conferred by a national patent

1. The rights conferred by a national patent in a Contracting State shall not extend to acts concerning a product covered by that patent which are done within the territory of that Contracting State after that product has been put on the market in any Contracting State by the proprietor of the patent or with his express consent, unless there are grounds which, under Community law, would justify the extension to such acts of the rights conferred by the patent.

Article 81 (continued)

2. Paragraph 1 shall also apply with regard to a product put on the market by the proprietor of a national patent, granted for the same invention in another Contracting State, who has economic connections with the proprietor of the patent referred to in paragraph 1. For the purpose of this paragraph, two persons shall be deemed to have economic connections where one of them is in a position to exert a decisive influence on the other, directly or indirectly, with regard to the exploitation of a patent, or where a third party is in a position to exercise such an influence on both persons.

3. The preceding paragraphs shall not apply in the case of a product put on the market under a compulsory licence.

Article 82
Compulsory licences in respect of national patents

Article 47 shall apply mutatis mutandis to the grant of compulsory licences for lack or insufficiency of exploitation of a national patent.

Article 83
Effect of unpublished
national applications or patents

1. Where Article 37 paragraph 2 applies, the Community patent shall be ineffective in the Contracting State concerned to the extent that it covers the same invention as the national patent application or patent.

2. The procedure confirming that, pursuant to paragraph 1, the Community patent is ineffective in the Contracting State shall, in that State, be that according to which, if the Community patent had been a national patent, it could have been revoked or made ineffective.

Article 84
National utility models and utility certificates

1. Articles 37, 80 and 81 shall apply to utility models and utility certificates and to applications for utility models and utility certificates in the Contracting States whose laws make provision for such models or certificates.

Article 84 (continued)

2. If a Contracting State provides in its law that a person may not exercise the rights conferred by a patent so long as there exists a utility model having an earlier date of filing or, where priority has been claimed, an earlier date of priority, the same shall, notwithstanding paragraph 1, apply also to the Community patent in that State.

PART VIII

TRANSITIONAL PROVISIONS

Article 85
Application of the Convention
on Jurisdiction and Enforcement

The provisions of the Convention on Jurisdiction and Enforcement rendered applicable by the preceding Articles shall not have effect in respect of any Contracting State for which that Convention has not yet entered into force until such entry into force.

Article 86
Option between a Community patent
and a European patent

1. This Convention shall, subject to paragraph 3, not apply to a European patent application filed during a transitional period nor to any resulting European patent, provided that the request for grant contains a statement that the applicant does not wish to obtain a Community patent. This statement may not be withdrawn.

Article 86 (continued)

2. Article 54 paragraphs 3 and 4 of the European Patent Convention shall apply where a European patent application in which the Contracting States are designated or a Community patent has a date of filing or, where priority has been claimed, a date of priority later than that of a European patent application in which one or some of the Contracting States are designated. In the event of limitation or revocation of the Community patent on this ground, limitation or revocation shall be pronounced only in respect of the Contracting States designated in the earlier European patent application as published.

3. Articles 80 to 82 and 84 shall apply to a European patent as referred to in paragraph 1, the references in Articles 80 and 84 to a Community patent and the references in Articles 81 and 82 to a national patent being understood as references to such a European patent.

4. The transitional period referred to in paragraph 1 may be terminated by decision of the Council of the European Communities, acting on a proposal from the Commission of the European Communities or from a Contracting State.

5. The decision referred to in paragraph 4 shall require unanimity.

Article 87
Subsequent choice of a Community patent

1. This Convention shall apply to a European patent granted in respect of a European patent application in which all the Contracting States are designated and which is filed prior to the entry into force of this Convention, provided that prior to the expiry of the time limit mentioned in Article 97 paragraph 2(b) of the European Patent Convention the applicant files with the European Patent Office a written statement that he wishes to obtain a Community patent.

/2. When this Convention takes effect with respect to a State after its entry into force, paragraph 1 shall apply *mutatis mutandis* to European patent applications to which this Convention applies and in which that State is designated./[10]

Article 88
Reservation concerning the translation of the specification of a Community patent

1. Notwithstanding Article 14 paragraph 9 any signatory State may, at the time of signature or when depositing its instrument of ratification, declare that it reserves the right to provide that, if the specification of a Community patent has been published in a language which is not one of the official languages of that State, the proprietor of the patent may, subject to the following paragraphs, avail himself, in that State, of the rights conferred by that patent, only under the condition that he files with the European Patent Office a translation of the specification, except for the claims, in one of the official languages of that State.

---
[10] The text in square brackets will be maintained in the event of the Agreement relating to Community Patents entering into force with fewer than twelve ratifications.

Article 88 (continued)

2. If the translation is filed within three months of the date of publication of the mention of the grant of the patent, the proprietor of the patent may avail himself from that date of the rights conferred by the patent.

3. If the translation is filed after the period referred to in paragraph 2, the proprietor of the patent may avail himself of the rights conferred by the patent from the date of filing of the translation. In respect of use of the invention without his consent in the period between the date of the publication of the mention of the grant of the patent and the date of filing of the translation, the proprietor may avail himself of the rights conferred by the patent only to the extent that he may, after the filing of the translation, claim reasonable compensation.

4. If the translation is filed more than three years after the expiry of the period mentioned in Article 99 paragraph 1 of the European Patent Convention, any person who has used or made effective and serious preparations for using the invention, within the period mentioned in paragraph 3 second sentence may continue use of the invention upon reasonable terms.

5. Any reservation made by a signatory State under paragraph 1 shall cease to apply when the Council of the European Communities, acting unanimously on a proposal from the Commission of the European Communities or from a signatory State, decides to terminate it. /The Council may only take such a decision after the Agreement relating to Community Patents has entered into force with respect to all the signatory States./[11]

---

[11] The text in square brackets will be maintained in the event of the Agreement relating to Community Patents entering into force with fewer than twelve ratifications.

Article 88 (continued)

6. Any signatory State that has made a reservation under paragraph 1 may withdrawn it at any time. Such withdrawal shall be made by notification addressed to the Secretary-General of the Council of the European Communities and shall take effect one month from the date of receipt of such notification.

7. Termination of the effect of the reservation shall not apply to Community patents granted before the date on which the reservation ceased to have effect.

Article 89
Reservation in respect of compulsory licences

1. Any signatory State may, at the time of signature or when depositing its instrument of ratification, declare that it reserves the right to provide that Articles 47 and 82 shall not apply within its territory to Community patents or to European patents granted for, or to national patents granted by, that State.

2. Any reservation made by a signatory State under paragraph 1 shall have effect until the end of the tenth year at the latest after the entry into force of the Agreement relating to Community Patents /with respect to all the signatory States./[12] However, the Council of the European Communities may, acting by a qualified majority on a proposal from a signatory State, extend the period in respect of a signatory State making such a reservation by not more than five years. This majority shall be that specified in the second indent of the second subparagraph of Article 148 paragraph 2 of the Treaty establishing the European Economic Community.

---
[12] The text in square brackets will be maintained in the event of the Agreement relating to Community Patents entering into force with fewer than twelve ratifications.

Article 89 (continued)

3. Any reservation made under paragraph 1 shall cease to apply when common rules on the granting of compulsory licences in respect of Community patents have become operative.

4. Any signatory State that has made a reservation under paragraph 1 may withdraw it at any time. Such withdrawal shall be made by notification addressed to the Secretary-General of the Council of the European Communities and shall take effect one month from the date of receipt of such notification.

5. Termination of the effect of the reservation shall not affect compulsory licences granted before the date on which the reservation ceased to have effect.

Article 90
Reservation in respect of infringement proceedings

- deleted -

Article 91
Other transitional provisions

1. Articles 159, 161 and 163 of the European Patent Convention shall apply <u>mutatis mutandis</u>, subject to the following:

   (a) the first meeting of the Select Committee of the Administrative Council shall be on the invitation of the Secretary-General of the Council of the European Communities;

   (b) the term "Contracting States" shall be understood as meaning the States parties to this Convention.

2. Notwithstanding paragraph 1(b), Article 64 paragraph 2 shall apply.

PART IX

FINAL PROVISIONS

Article 92
Implementing Regulations

1. The Implementing Regulations shall be an integral part of this Convention.

2. In the case of conflict between the provisions of this Convention and those of the Implementing Regulations, the provisions of this Convention shall prevail.

Article 93

Precedence of the provisions of the Treaty establishing the European Economic Community

- deleted -

Article 94

Ratification

- deleted -

Article 95

Accession

- deleted -

Article 96

Participation of third States

- deleted -

Article 97

Territorial field of application

- deleted -

Article 98
Entry into force

– deleted –

Article 99
Duration of the Convention

– deleted –

Article 100
Revision

– deleted –

Article 101
Disputes between Contracting States

– deleted –

Article 102
Original of the Convention

– deleted –

Article 103
Notification

– deleted –

**IMPLEMENTING REGULATIONS
TO THE CONVENTION FOR THE EUROPEAN PATENT
FOR THE COMMON MARKET**

PART I
IMPLEMENTING REGULATIONS TO PART I OF THE CONVENTION

CHAPTER I

Organisation of the special departments

Rule 1
Allocation of duties to the departments of the first instance

1. The President of the European Patent Office shall determine the number of Revocation Divisions. He shall allocate duties to these departments by reference to the international classification.

2. The President of the European Patent Office shall, with the agreement of the Select Committee of the Administrative Council, determine in detail the duties for which the Patent Administration Division is responsible pursuant to Article 8.

3. In addition to the responsibilities vested in them under the Convention, the President of the European Patent Office may allocate further duties to the Patent Administration Division and the Revocation Divisions.

4. The President of the European Patent Office may entrust to employees who are not technically or legally qualified members the execution of individual duties falling to the Patent Administration Division or the Revocation Divisions, and involving no technical or legal difficulties.

Rule 2
Allocation of duties to the departments of the second instance and designation of their members

– deleted –

Rule 3
Rules of Procedure of the Revocation Boards

– deleted –

Rule 4
Administrative structure of the special departments

1. The Revocation Divisions may be grouped together administratively with the Examining Divisions and Opposition Divisions so as to form Directorates, or may form a Directorate together with the Patent Administration Division.

2. The special departments may be grouped together administratively with other departments of the European Patent Office so as to form Directorates-General or may form a separate Directorate-General; in the latter case, Rule 12 paragraph 3 of the Implementing Regulations to the European Patent Convention shall apply, but the appointment of a Vice-President to the Directorate-General shall be decided upon by the Select Committee of the Administrative Council.

CHAPTER II

Languages of the special departments

Rule 5
Language of the proceedings

1. Rules 1 to 3, Rule 5, Rule 6 paragraph 2 and Rule 7 of the Implementing Regulations to the European Patent Convention shall apply _mutatis mutandis_ to proceedings before the special departments.

2. A reduction in the limitation fee, revocation fee or appeal fee shall be allowed the proprietor of a patent or an applicant for revocation who avails himself of the options provided for in Article 14 paragraph 4. The reduction shall be fixed in the Rules relating to Fees at a percentage of the total of the fees.

PART II

IMPLEMENTING REGULATIONS TO PART II
OF THE CONVENTION

Rule 6
Suspension of proceedings

Rule 13 of the Implementing Regulations to the European Patent Convention shall apply _mutatis mutandis_ to limitation proceedings and revocation proceedings.

Rule 7
Entries regarding claims to the right to Community patents

The entries referred to in Article 27 paragraph 4 shall be made:

(a) at the request of the registrar of the court before which the proceedings are instituted;

(b) at the request of the claimant or any other interested person.

Rule 8
Request to file translations of the claims in examination or opposition proceedings

1. The European Patent Office shall request the applicant for or proprietor of the patent to file, within three months, the translations prescribed in Article 33 paragraphs 1 and 2 and to pay the fee for the publication of the translations of the claims within the same period.

2. The request shall be sent at the same time as:

   (a) in the case of examination proceedings, the request referred to in Rule 51 paragraph 4 of the Implementing Regulations to the European Patent Convention;

   (b) in the case of opposition proceedings, the request referred to in Rule 58 paragraph 5 of the Implementing Regulations to the European Patent Convention.

3. The further period referred to in Article 33 paragraph 5 shall be two months.

Rule 9
Correction of the translation

1. Where Article 33 paragraphs 1 and 2 apply, the applicant for or proprietor of the patent may file at the European Patent Office a corrected translation for the purposes of publication. The corrected translation shall not be deemed to have been filed until the fee for its publication has been paid.

2. Where a Contracting State has adopted a provision pursuant to Article 34 paragraph 2, the applicant whose translation of the claims has been published, may file with the competent authority of that State a corrected translation for the purposes of publication.

Rule 10
Registering transfers, licences and other rights

1. Rules 20 to 22 of the Implementing Regulations to the European Patent Convention shall apply *mutatis mutandis* to entries made in the Register of Community Patents.

2. The request provided for in Article 28 paragraph 2 must, in the case of subparagraph (a), be made within two months, or in the case of subparagraph (b), within four months, of receipt of notification from the European Patent Office that the name of a new proprietor has been entered in the Register of Community Patents.

Rule 10 (continued)

3. Where a Community patent is involved in bakruptcy or like proceedings, an entry to this effect shall be made in the Register of Community Patents on request of the competent national authority. The entry shall not incur a fee.

4. The entry referred to in paragraph 3 shall be deleted at the request of the competent national authority. The request shall not incur a fee.

5. Where a European patent application in which the Contracting States are designated is involved in bankruptcy or like proceedings, paragraphs 3 and 4 shall apply mutatis mutandis but the reference to the Register of Community Patents shall be understood as being a reference to the Register of European Patents provided for in the European Patent Convention.

Rule 11
Licences of right

1. Any person who wishes to use the invention after a statement provided for in Article 44 paragraph 1 has been filed, shall declare his intention to the proprietor of the patent by registered letter. The declaration shall be deemed to have been made one week after posting of the registered letter. A copy of this declaration, stating the date upon which the declaration was posted, shall be sent to the European Patent Office. Failing this, the European Patent Office shall, in the event of withdrawal of the statement, consider the declaration not to have been made.

Rule 11 (continued)

2. The declaration shall state how the invention is to be used. After the declaration has been made, the person making it shall be entitled to use the invention in the way he has stated.

3. The licensee shall be obliged at the end of every quarter of a calendar year to report to the proprietor of the patent on the use made thereof and to pay the compensation therefor. If this obligation is not complied with, the proprietor of the patent may lay down a further suitable time limit for this purpose. If the time limit is not complied with the licence shall expire.

4. A request for review of the compensation determined by the Revocation Division may be made only after the expiry of one year from the last determination of compensation.

PART III

**IMPLEMENTING REGULATIONS TO PART III
OF THE CONVENTION**

CHAPTER I

Renewal fees

Rule 12
Payment of renewal fees

1. Rule 37 paragraphs 1 and 2 of the Implementing Regulations to the European Patent Convention shall apply to the payment of renewal fees for Community patents.

2. An additional fee shall be deemed to have been paid at the same time as the renewal fee within the meaning of Article 49 paragraph 2 if it is paid within the period laid down in that provision.

Rule 13
Period for the entry of surrender

The period referred to in Article 50 paragraph 3 shall be three months from the date on which the proprietor of the patent has proved to the European Patent Office that he has informed the licensee of his intention to surrender. If, before expiry of the period, the proprietor of the patent proves to the European Patent Office that the licensee agrees to the surrender, it may be entered immediately.

CHAPTER II

Limitation procedure

Rule 14
Period for the filing
of the request for limitation

Rule 13 shall apply *mutatis mutandis* to the filing of the request for limitation of the Community patent.

Rule 15
Content of the request for limitation

The request for limitation of a Community patent shall contain:

(a) the number of the Community patent which it is sought to limit, the name of the proprietor and the title of the invention;

(b) the amendments sought;

(c) if the proprietor of the patent has appointed a representative, his name and the address of his place of business in accordance with Rule 26 paragraph 2(c) of the Implementing Regulations to the European Patent Convention.

Rule 16
Rejection of the request for limitation
ad inadmissible

If the Revocation Division notes that the request for limitation of a Community patent does not comply with Article 52 paragraphs 1 and 3 and Rule 15, it shall communicate this to the proprietor of the patent and shall invite him to remedy the deficiencies noted within such a period as it may specify. If the request for limitation is not corrected in good time, the Revocation Division shall reject it as inadmissible.

Rule 17
Examination of the request for limitation

1. If the request for limitation of the Community patent is admissible, the proprietor of the patent shall, in any communication pursuant to Article 53 paragraph 2, where appropriate, be invited to file the description, claims and drawings in amended form.

2. Where necessary, any communication pursuant to Article 53 paragraph 2 shall contain a reasoned statement. Where appropriate, this statement shall cover all the grounds against the limitation of the patent.

3. Before the Revocation Division decides on the limitation of the patent, it shall inform the proprietor of the extent to which it intends to limit the patent, and shall request him to pay within three months the fee for printing a new patent specification and to file the translations prescribed in Article 54 paragraph 2(b) within the same period. If within that period the proprietor has communicated his disapproval of the patent being limited to this extent, the communication of the Revocation Division shall be deemed not to have been made, and the limitation proceedings shall be resumed.

Rule 17 (continued)

4. The further period referred to in Article 54 paragraph 3 shall be two months.

5. The decision to limit the patent shall state the text of the patent as limited.

Rule 18
Resumption of limitation proceedings

Where limitation proceedings have been stayed because of revocation proceedings which result in a decision under Article 59 paragraph 2 or 3, the Revocation Division, after the publication of the mention of such decision, shall communicate to the proprietor of the patent that the proceedings will be resumed after notification of this communication to the proprietor. Rule 13 paragraph 5 of the Implementing Regulations to the European Patent Convention shall apply mutatis mutandis.

Rule 19
Different claims, description and drawings
in the case of limitation

Where it is decided to limit a Community patent in respect of one or some of the Contracting States, the Community patent may, where appropriate, contain, for that State or States, claims and, if the Revocation Division considers it necessary, a description and drawings which are different from those for the other Contracting States.

Rule 20
Form of the new specification
following limitation proceedings

The President of the European Patent Office shall prescribe the form of the publication of the new specification of the Community patent and the data which are to be included.

CHAPTER III

Revocation procedure

Rule 21
Content of the application for revocation

An application for revocation of a Community patent shall contain:

(a) the name and address of the applicant for revocation and the State in which his residence or principal place of business is located, in accordance with Rule 26 paragraph 2(c) of the Implementing Regulations to the European Patent Convention;

(b) the number of the patent in respect of which revocation is applied for, the name of the proprietor and the title of the invention;

(c) a statement of the extent to which revocation is applied for and of the grounds on which the application is based as well as an indication of the facts, evidence and arguments presented in support of these grounds;

(d) if the applicant has appointed a representative, his name and the address of his place of business, in accordance with Rule 26 paragraph 2(c) of the Implementing Regulations to the European Patent Convention.

Rule 22
Security for the costs of proceedings

The security for the costs of the proceedings shall be deposited in a currency in which fees may be paid. It must be deposited with a financial or banking establishment included in the list drawn up by the President of the European Patent Office. The national law of the Contracting State in which the establishment has its place of business shall apply to any such security.

Rule 23
Rejection of the application for revocation as inadmissible

1. The Revocation Division shall communicate the application for revocation to the proprietor of the patent who may comment on its admissibility within one month.

2. If the Revocation Division notes that the application for revocation does not comply with Article 56 paragraphs 1 and 4, Rule 21 and Rule 5 of these Implementing Regulations in conjunction with Rule 1 paragraph 1 of the Implementing Regulations to the European Patent Convention, it shall communicate this to the proprietor and to the applicant and shall invite the applicant to remedy the deficiencies noted within such period as it may specify. If the application for revocation is not corrected in good time, the Revocation Division shall reject it as inadmissible.

3. Any decision to reject an application for revocation as inadmissible shall be communicated to the proprietor of the patent.

Rule 24
Preparation of the examination
of the application for revocation

1. If the application for revocation is admissible, the Revocation Division shall invite the proprietor of the patent to file his observations and to file amendments, where appropriate, to the description, claims and drawings within a period to be fixed by the Revocation Division.

2. The observations and any amendments filed by the proprietor of the patent shall be communicated to the applicant who shall be invited by the Revocation Division, if it considers it expedient, to reply within a period to be fixed by the Revocation Division.

Rule 25
Examination of the application for revocation

1. All communications issued pursuant to Article 58 paragraph 2 and all replies thereto shall be communicated to all parties.

2. In any communication from the Revocation Division to the proprietor of the patent pursuant to Article 58 paragraph 2, he shall, where appropriate, be invited to file the description, claims and drawings in amended form.

3. Where necessary, any communication from the Revocation Division to the proprietor of the patent pursuant to Article 58 paragraph 2 shall contain a reasoned statement. Where appropriate, this statement shall cover all the grounds against the maintenance of the Community patent.

Rule 25 (continued)

4. Before the Revocation Division decides on the maintenance of the patent in the amended form, it shall inform the parties that it intends to maintain the patent as amended and shall invite them to state their observations within a period of one month if they disapprove of the text in which it is intended to maintain the patent.

5. If disapproval of the text communicated by the Revocation Division is expressed, examination of the revocation may be continued; otherwise, the Revocation Division shall, on expiry of the period referred to in paragraph 4, request the proprietor of the patent to pay within three months the fee for the printing of a new specification and, if the claims are amended, to file the translations prescribed in Article 59 paragraph 3(b) within the same period.

6. The further period referred to in Article 59 paragraph 4 shall be two months.

7. The decision to maintain the patent as amended shall state which text of the patent forms the basis for the maintenance thereof.

Rule 26
Joint processing of applications for revocation

1. The Revocation Division may order that two or more applications for revocation pending before it and relating to the same Community patent, be dealt with jointly in order to carry out a joint investigation and take a joint decision.

2. The Revocation Division may rescind an order given pursuant to paragraph 1.

Rule 27
Different claims, description and drawings
in the case of revocation

Where revocation of a Community patent is pronounced in respect of one or more of the Contracting States, Rule 19 shall apply *mutatis mutandis*.

Rule 28
Form of the new specification
following revocation proceedings

Rule 20 shall apply to the new specification of the Community patent referred to in Article 60.

Rule 29
Other provisions applicable to revocation
proceedings

Rules 59, 60 and 63 of the Implementing Regulations to the European Patent Convention shall apply *mutatis mutandis* to requests for documents, continuation of revocation proceedings by the European Patent Office of its own motion and costs in revocation proceedings.

PART IV

IMPLEMENTING REGULATIONS TO PART IV OF THE CONVENTION

Rule 30
Appeal proceedings

– deleted –

PART V

IMPLEMENTING REGULATIONS TO PART V OF THE CONVENTION

Rule 31
Entries in the Register of Community Patents

1. Rule 92 paragraphs 1(a) to (l), (o), (q) to (u) and (w), 2 and 3 of the Implementing Regulations to the European Patent Convention shall apply mutatis mutandis to the Register of Community Patents.

2. The Register of Community Patents shall also contain the following entries:

Rule 31 (continued)

(a) date of lapse of the Community patent in the cases provided for in Article 51 paragraph 1(b) and (c);

(b) date of filing of the statement provided for in Article 44;

(c) date of receipt of a request for limitation of the Community patent;

(d) date and purport of the decision on the request for limitation of the Community patent;

(e) date of receipt of an application for revocation of the Community patent;

(f) date and purport of the decision on the application for revocation of the Community patent;

(g) particulars of matters referred to in Article 27 paragraph 4;

(h) a record of the information communicated to the European Patent Office concerning proceedings under the Protocol on Litigation.

Rule 32
Additional publications by the European Patent Office

The President of the European Patent Office shall determine in what form the translations of claims filed pursuant to the Convention by the applicant for or proprietor of a patent and, where appropriate, corrected translations, shall be published and whether particulars of such translations and corrected translations should be entered in the Community Patent Bulletin.

Rule 33
Other common provisions

Rules 36 and 106 and the provisions of Part VII of the Implementing Regulations to the European Patent Convention, with the exception of Rule 85 paragraph 3, Rules 86, 87, 92 and 96 shall apply _mutatis mutandis_ subject to the following:

(a) Rule 69 shall not apply to decisions on requests for limitation or on applications for revocation of the Community patent;

(b) the Select Committee of the Administrative Council shall determine the details of the application of Rule 74 paragraphs 2 and 3;

(c) the term "Contracting States" shall be understood as meaning the States parties to this Convention.

PART VI

IMPLEMENTING REGULATIONS TO PART VIII OF THE CONVENTION

Rule 34
Forwarding of translations

The European Patent Office shall enter in the Register of Community Patents the date on which a translation pursuant to Article 88 is filed and shall, as soon as possible, forward a copy of the translation to the central industrial property office of the Contracting State concerned.

PROTOCOL
CONFERRING POWERS IN RESPECT OF COMMUNITY PATENTS
ON CERTAINS INSTITUTIONS
OF THE EUROPEAN COMMUNITIES

/PROTOCOL
CONFERRING POWERS IN RESPECT OF COMMUNITY PATENTS
ON CERTAIN INSTITUTIONS
OF THE EUROPEAN COMMUNITIES

THE HIGH CONTRACTING PARTIES to the Treaty establishing the European Economic Community,

HAVING REGARD to the fact that the Agreement relating to Community Patents signed at ..... on .... may enter into force once it has been ratified by ..... ,

CONSIDERING that the final objective remains the implementation of the Community patent system in respect of all the Member States of the European Economic Community,

CONSIDERING that the operation of the system established by the Agreement relating to Community Patents requires that certain Institutions of the European Communities be given powers in respect of Community patents, even before that Agreement is in force in respect of all the Member States of the European Economic Community,

CONSIDERING that it is essential that no provision of the Agreement relating to Community Patents be invoked against the application of the Treaty establishing the European Economic Community and that appropriate jurisdiction be conferred on the Court of Justice of the European Communities as from the entry into force of that Agreement in order to ensure the uniformity of the Community legal order,

HAVE DECIDED to conclude this Protocol and to this end have designated as their Plenipotentiaries:

HIS MAJESTY THE KING OF THE BELGIANS:

HER MAJESTY THE QUEEN OF DENMARK:

THE PRESIDENT OF THE FEDERAL REPUBLIC OF GERMANY:

THE PRESIDENT OF THE HELLENIC REPUBLIC:

HIS MAJESTY THE KING OF SPAIN:

THE PRESIDENT OF THE FRENCH REPUBLIC:

THE PRESIDENT OF IRELAND:

THE PRESIDENT OF THE ITALIAN REPUBLIC:

HIS ROYAL HIGHNESS THE GRAND DUKE OF LUXEMBOURG:

HER MAJESTY THE QUEEN OF THE NETHERLANDS:

THE PRESIDENT OF THE PORTUGUESE REPUBLIC:

HER MAJESTY THE QUEEN OF THE UNITED KINGDOM OF GREAT BRITAIN AND NORTHERN IRELAND:

WHO, meeting in the Council of the European Communities, having exchanged their full powers, found in good and due form,

HAVE AGREED AS FOLLOWS:

Article 1

1. The Court of Justice of the European Communities shall in respect of Community patents have the jurisdiction conferred on it by the Agreement relating to Community Patents signed at ...... on .... The Protocol on the Statute of the Court of Justice of the European Economic Community and the Rules of Procedure of the Court of Justice shall apply.

2. The Rules of Procedure shall be adapted and supplemented, as necessary, in conformity with Article 188 of the Treaty establishing the European Economic Community.

Article 2

The other Institutions of the European Communities referred to in the Agreement relating to Community Patents shall exercise the powers conferred on them by that Agreement.

Article 3

This Protocol shall be subject to ratification by the signatory States; instruments of ratification shall be deposited with the Secretary-General of the Council of the European Communities.

Article 4

This Protocol shall enter into force on the first day of the third month following the deposit of the instrument of ratification by the last signatory State to take this step.

Article 5

This Protocol, drawn up in a single original in the Danish, Dutch, English, French, German, Greek, Irish, Italian, Portuguese and Spanish languages, all ten texts being equally authentic, shall be deposited in the archives of the General Secretariat of the Council of the European Communities. The Secretary-General shall transmit a certified copy to the Government of each Member State of the European Economic Community.

IN WITNESS WHEREOF, the undersigned Plenipotentiaries have affixed their signatures below this Protocol.

Done at .... on........... /[13]

---
[13] This Protocol will be maintained in the event of the Agreement relating to Community Patents entering into force with fewer than twelve ratifications.

JOINT DECLARATION

JOINT DECLARATION

Upon signature of the Agreement relating to Community Patents, the Governments of the Kingdom of Belgium, the Kingdom of Denmark, the Federal Republic of Germany, the Hellenic Republic, the Kingdom of Spain, the French Republic, Ireland, the Italian Republic, the Grand Duchy of Luxembourg, the Kingdom of the Netherlands, the Portuguese Republic and the United Kingdom of Great Britain and Northern Ireland:

1. Confirm their agreement to the Resolution concerning prior use or possession, to the Resolution on common rules on the granting of compulsory licences in respect of Community patents and to the Decision on preparations for the commencement of the activities of the special departments of the European Patent Office, as annexed to the Final Act of the 1975 Luxembourg Conference on the Community Patent;

2. Record their agreement to the following Declarations and Decision, as annexed hereto:

    - Declaration on the adjustment of national patent law;

    - Declaration on the operation of the Common Appeal Court during a transitional period;

    - Supplementary Decision to the Decision on preparations for the commencement of the activities of the special departments of the European Patent Office.

In witness whereof the undersigned, duly empowered to that end, have signed this Joint Declaration.

Done at .... on ....

DECLARATION
ON THE ADJUSTMENT OF NATIONAL PATENT LAW[14]

THE GOVERNMENTS OF THE MEMBER STATES OF THE EUROPEAN ECONOMIC COMMUNITY,

Upon signature of the Agreement relating to Community Patents,

Noting that since the signing of the Community Patent Convention of 15 December 1975 legislative procedures have been completed in several Member States with a view to eliminating as far as possible the differences between national patent law and the common system of law for patents resulting from the said Convention,

TAKE NOTE of the undertaking by the Government of each Member State in which these procedures have not been completed or are yet to be begun to endeavour to adjust its law relating to national patents so as to bring it into conformity, as far as practicable, with corresponding provisions of the European Patent Convention, the Agreement relating to Community Patents and the Patent Cooperation Treaty.

---
[14] On initialling the texts established by the Conference, the Representative of the Government of the Hellenic Republic stated that this initialling did not cover this Declaration.

DECLARATION
ON THE OPERATION OF THE COMMON APPEAL COURT
DURING A TRANSITIONAL PERIOD

THE GOVERNMENTS OF THE MEMBER STATES OF THE EUROPEAN ECONOMIC COMMUNITY,

Upon signature of the Agreement relating to Community Patents and, in particular, of the Protocol on the Settlement of Litigation concerning the Infringement and Validity of Community Patents,

Considering that, during a period of unforeseeable duration, the revenue derived from renewal fees for the Community patent will be less than the cost of the additional tasks entrusted to the European Patent Office and the expenditure resulting from the operation of the Common Appeal Court,

EXPRESS their firm intention to make every effort to ensure that, during this period, the Common Appeal Court is set up progressively, with its members being paid on the basis of the number of cases brought before it and staff being recruited in line with the increase in requirements,

RECOMMEND the Administrative Committee to take these objectives into account in the decisions it takes, in particular pursuant to Article 11 of the Protocol on the Settlement of Litigation concerning the Infringement and Validity of Community Patents.

SUPPLEMENTARY DECISION
TO THE DECISION ON PREPARATIONS
FOR THE COMMENCEMENT OF THE ACTIVITIES OF THE SPECIAL DEPARTMENTS
OF THE EUROPEAN PATENT OFFICE

THE GOVERNMENTS OF THE MEMBER STATES OF THE EUROPEAN ECONOMIC COMMUNITY,

Upon signature of the Agreement relating to Community Patents,

Having regard to the Decision of 15 December 1975 on preparations for the commencement of the activities of the special departments of the European Patent Office,

HAVE ADOPTED THE FOLLOWING DECISION:

1. The last sentence of the first paragraph of the Decision on preparations for the commencement of the activities of the special departments of the European Patent Office shall be replaced by the following:

    "The duty of the Interim Committee to prepare for the commencement of the activities of the special departments of the European Patent Office shall cease when the Select Committee of the Administrative Council meets pursuant to Article 91 paragraph 1(a) of the Community Patent Convention. The Interim Committee shall be disbanded when the Administrative Committee of the Common Appeal Court meets for the first time."

2. It shall also be the duty of the Interim Committee to take all preparatory measures to enable the Common Appeal Court to begin its activities in due time.

3. The preparations for the commencement of the activities of the Common Appeal Court may be carried out by Working Parties.

European Communities — Council

Texts established by the Luxembourg Conference on the Community patent, 1985

Luxembourg: Office for Official Publications of the European Communities

1986 — 214 pp. — 21 × 29.7 cm

DA, DE, GR, EN, ES, FR, IT, NL, PT

ISBN : 92-824-0312-2

Catalogue number: BX-45-86-814-EN-C

Price (excluding VAT) in Luxembourg
ECU 11.21   BFR 500   IRL 8.10   UKL 7   USD 10